D0595861

SCHOLASTIQUE MUKASONGA

Cockroaches

Translated from the French
by Jordan Stump

archipelago books

Archipelago Books
232 Third St. #A111
Brooklyn, NY 11215
www.archipelagobooks.org

Library of Congress Cataloging-in-Publication Data
Mukasonga, Scholastique, author. | Stump, Jordan, 1959- translator.
Cockroaches / Scholastique Mukasonga ; translated by Jordan Stump.
[Inyenzi, ou, Les cafards. English]
Brooklyn, NY : Archipelago, 2016.
LCCN 2016025248 | ISBN 9780914671534 (paperback)
LCC DT450.443.M8513 A3 2016 | DDC 967.57104/31 [B] --dc23
LLC record available at https://lccn.loc.gov/2016025248

Distributed by Penguin Random House
www.penguinrandomhouse.com

Cover art: Cai Guo-Qiang

Cet ouvrage a bénéficié du soutien des Programmes d'aides à la publication de l'Institut Français.

This work, published as part of a program of aid for publication,
received support from the Institut Français.

Cet ouvrage a bénéficié du soutien du Ministère des Affaires étrangères et
du Service Culturel de l'Ambassade de France aux Etats-Unis.

This work received support from the French Ministry of Foreign Affairs and
the Cultural Services of the French Embassy in the United States.

Archipelago Books is grateful for the generous support of the Lannan Foundation,
the National Endowment for the Arts, the New York City Department of Cultural Affairs,
and the New York State Council on the Arts, a state agency.

Cockroaches

For everyone who died at Nyamata in the genocide,
for Cosma, my father,
for Stefania, my mother,
for Antoine, my brother, and his nine children,
for Alexia, my sister, and her husband, Pierre Ntereye,
    and their children,
for Jeanne, my youngest sister, and her children,
for Judith and Julienne, my sisters, and their children,

for all those of Nyamata who are named in this book and
    all the many more who are not,

for the few who have the sorrow of surviving.

Every night the same nightmare interrupts my sleep. I'm being chased, I hear a sort of hum coming toward me, a roar, more menacing with every moment. I don't look back. There's no need. I know who's chasing me . . . I know they have machetes. I'm not sure how, but even without looking back I know they have machetes . . . Sometimes the other girls from school are there too. I hear their cries as they fall. As they . . . Now I'm the only one running, I know I'm going to fall, I'm going to be trampled, I don't want to feel the cold blade on my neck, I . . .

I wake up. I'm in France. The house is silent. My children are asleep in their room. Peacefully. I turn on the bedside lamp. I go into the main room and sit down at a little table. On it are a wooden box and a schoolchild's notebook with a blue cover. I don't need to open the box, I know what's inside: a piece of worn brick, a dried leaf, a flat tapered stone with sharp edges, letters written on pages torn from a notebook.

There's also a photograph on the table – a wedding photo, from my youngest sister Jeanne's wedding. We're all together: the bride in the white gown I'd ordered from a Pakistani tailor in Bujumbura, and Emmanuel, the groom, in his tight-fitting suit, and my father with his white *pagne* knotted over his shoulder, and my very frail mother in her Sunday best. I look for my oldest brother Antoine and his nine children, and my big sister Alexia and her husband Pierre Ntereye, a university professor, and Judith, the oldest child, who made the food for the festivities because she'd learned "modern" cuisine in Kigali, and all the nephews and nieces and everyone from Nyamata, from Gitwe, from Gitagata. They're going to die. Maybe they already know it.

Where are they now? In the memorial crypt of the church in Nyamata, nameless skulls among all the other bones? In the bush, beneath the brambles, in some mass grave that has yet to be found? Over and over, I write and rewrite their names in the blue-covered notebook, trying to prove to myself that they existed; I speak their names one by one, in the dark and the silence. I have to fix a face on each name, hang some shred of a memory. I don't want to cry, I feel tears running down my cheeks. I close my eyes. This will be another sleepless night. I have so many dead to sit up with.

The late 1950s:
A childhood disturbed

I was born in the southwest of Rwanda, in Gikongoro province, at the edge of Nyungwe forest, a large high-altitude rainforest, supposedly home – but has anyone ever seen them? – to the last African forest elephants. My parents' enclosure was in Cyanika, by the river Rukarara.

Of my birthplace I have no memory but the homesick stories my mother told all through our exile in Nyamata. She missed the wheat she could grow at that altitude, and the gruel she could make with it. She told us of her battles with the aggressive monkeys that ravaged the fields she farmed with her mattock. "Sometimes, when I was young," she would say, "I joined the little shepherds tending the cows at the edge of the forest. Often the monkeys attacked us. They walked on two feet, just like men. They wouldn't put up with my little friends' insolence. They attacked them. They wanted to show them that monkeys are stronger than men."

My father was not an aristocrat with vast herds of cows, as some people think of the Tutsis. Still, he knew how to read and write, and he'd learned Kiswahili, the language used by the colonial administration, so he worked as an accountant and secretary to sub-chief Ruvebana. But he was a real jack of all trades: he managed his boss's assets, and when it was necessary he went to prison in his boss's place. He was serving a sentence for him when my oldest sister Alexia was born. That earned her the slightly odd name of Ntabyerangode: "Nothing-is-ever-completely-white." Which, to my father, meant that the joy of his daughter's birth had been somewhat spoiled by his incarceration. Sometimes, too, my father Cosma went hunting for gold in the torrents of the mountains on the Congolese border. He came home with a few little chips, in matchboxes. We never got rich off those tiny flakes.

In 1958, sub-chief Ruvebana was appointed to Butare province, and my family followed him. The sub-chiefdom was located in the far south of the province, on the crests overlooking the valley of the Kanyaru, whose course forms the border with Burundi. From our new house, in Magi, on the steep foothills of Mount Makwaza, we had a sweeping view: the valley of the Kanyaru and its papyrus swamps, and, beyond, much of the Ngozi province in Burundi.

Mount Makwaza was the homeland of a great Hutu chief, an *igihinza*. We were terribly afraid of him. My mother described him as a giant, always dressed in a leopard skin. When threatening clouds shrouded the mountaintop, she would tell us, "Someone must have angered the *igihinza*, be good now." In our childish terror, we believed the *igihinza*'s enormous shadow was darkening the whole mountainside. No one dared venture out at the foot of Mount Makwaza after dark, for fear of disturbing the *igihinza*'s nighttime doings. Up at the very top of the mountain, we thought we could see the glow of his fire.

My big sister Alexia and my older brothers Antoine and André went to school. My mother worked in the fields. We rarely saw my father at home; he had an office, which still exists, facing the subchief's residence, but he didn't spend much time there, because he was always out on his bicycle seeing to matters that I found deeply mysterious. My father had the only bicycle in the area, which gave him considerable prestige, reinforced by the pen sticking out of his shirt pocket, an uncontested sign of his authority. The moment they spotted him pedaling along the narrow mountain path, the village children would cry out "It's Cosma! It's Cosma!" and parade along beside him all the way to the house. Hearing those shouts, my mother would begin reheating the pot of beans and bananas she always kept ready for my father's unexpected returns. I can still picture that pot, reserved for my father's meals alone. It was tall, completely black but shiny inside, made of very thick cast iron. It was the only metal kitchenware we owned. It had a name: *Isafuriya ndende*, the "big cookpot." My father told of buying it from a street-merchant in Zanzibar. It was a very precious object, so precious that my mother wouldn't leave it behind when we were expelled from Magi. The famous cookpot followed us into our exile in Nyamata.

We were still living in a mud hut with a straw roof, but my father set about having a brick house built on our plot of land. He went into debt for it. My mother was apprehensive about moving into a house like the white people's, or almost – an *urutare*, a "big rock," as she called it. She still missed the warm intimacy of the hut she'd lived in as a child, a big hut made of artistically woven grasses.

As for me, I spent my days with the potters who'd set up their camp in the eucalyptus woods facing the house. They were Batwa, a people kept at arm's length by the rest of Rwanda. The first Europeans called them Pygmies, very wrongly. Boniface, the patriarch of the "tribe," welcomed me as if I were his own daughter, and my mother thought nothing of seeing me go off to play with the children of people traditionally treated as pariahs. She often gave me beans and sweet potatoes for the children, and in return the Batwa brought her their nicest pots.

The first pogroms against the Tutsis broke out on All Saints' Day, 1959. The machinery of the genocide had been set into motion. It would never stop. Until the final solution, it would never stop.

Needless to say, the anti-Tutsi violence didn't spare Butare province. I was three years old, and that was when the first images of terror were etched into my memory. I remember. My brothers and my sister were at school. I was at home with my mother. All at once we saw plumes of smoke everywhere, rising up from the slopes of Mount Makwaza, from the valley of the Rususa, where Ruvebana's mother Suzanne, who was like a grandmother to me, had a house. And then we heard noises, shouts, a hum like a swarm of monstrous bees, a growl filling the air. I can still hear that growl today, like a menace swelling behind me. Sometimes I hear that growl in France, in the street; I don't dare turn around, I walk faster, isn't it that same roar, forever following me?

My mother immediately lifted me onto her back: "Hurry, we've got to go get the children so they won't try to come home."

But just then a crowd appeared, bellowing, with machetes in their hands, and spears, bows, clubs, torches. We hurried to hide in the banana grove. Still roaring, the men burst into our house. They set fire to the straw-roofed hut, the stables full of calves. They slashed the stores of beans and sorghum. They launched a frenzied attack on the brick house we would never live in. They didn't take anything, they only wanted to destroy, to wipe out all sign of us, annihilate us.

They almost succeeded. Nothing remains of my parents' enclosure in Magi but a tall fig tree. I picked up a little fragment of brick from a pile of rubble – I'd like to think it came from our house. An old woman came running toward me from the banana grove, grumbling: Who is this stranger? What's she doing prowling around the hut? I said nothing, unable to break in with a question while she went on and on, as if talking to herself. Suddenly I heard her say the name Cosma. Cosma? Cosma, yes, she remembered him, or she'd heard about him. But she wasn't there the day my house was destroyed, she was sick, or maybe she was getting married. Why bring all that up again? It was so long ago. Had I come to drive her out of her little house?

I look at the tall fig tree. No, the killers hadn't succeeded. My two sons are alive. They've seen the tall fig tree that preserves the memories, and like that tree they'll remember.

I don't know how my mother managed to get Antoine, André, and Alexia from school. We were all gathered together in the sub-chief's enclosure. The Tutsi families that had escaped the slaughter and whose houses had been burned had spontaneously come there to seek refuge. I believe my father tried to organize the crowd as best he could. After nightfall, we set out for the Mugombwa mission.

My brother André says it was Belgian paratroopers who oversaw the transfer. "Just to keep us in line," he said, "one of them threw a grenade at a dog, and it was blown limb from limb." From then on the Tutsis knew where they stood.

The refugees were housed in Mugombwa church and the classrooms of the mission. They stayed there for some two weeks. In my little-girl mind, I found it all wonderful. There were many, many people. The mothers cooked in the courtyard. My brothers and my big sister no longer went off to school. My mother no longer tended to the crops. The children played all day long, and we ate something we never had at home: rice! It was strange, everyone slept on the floor in the same room, even the parents! I wasn't afraid anymore!

I went back to see the school buildings we'd been stuffed into. A far grander church was built next to them in 1976. In April 1994, the Tutsis took refuge there, or were driven there. I was told that Father Tiziano, as the people of Mugombwa called him, an Italian, locked the church doors with a padlock and fled to Burundi, declaring that everything would be fine. Today the tile roof, peppered with holes made by bullets and grenade shrapnel, has been replaced by a bold metal framework. On Sundays the church is full. How many murderers among the pious assembly? The faithful sing with all their hearts. Jesus is kind. He forgives all sins. He forgets everything. When Mass is over, the young people from a Catholic movement raise the

Vatican's gold and white flag, marked with the Chi-Rho symbol. Hand on heart, they sing a hymn to the glory of Saint Francis Xavier. Who would ever be so rude as to bring up the "unfortunate events," as they're called by those who deny all participation in the genocide and refuse to speak the word? Let us forgive each other, and let us go on as if nothing had happened.

——— ——— ———

While I was playing in front of the school, some odd things were going on in one of the classrooms. As my brother explained it, all the family heads were appearing by turns before a sort of jury of Hutu notables. They decided who could stay and who was to be expelled. As it happened, all the Tutsis whose houses had burned were to be banished. Maybe they wanted to be sure there were no stray Hutus among the exiles.

One morning, before dawn, they brought us out of the classrooms. The schoolyard was full of trucks. I'd never seen so many. The motors were running. Their headlights blinded us. We heard shouting: "Into the trucks, faster, faster!" There was no time to gather the few humble belongings we'd managed to bring with us. My mother brought only the famous black cast-iron cookpot. That was our only luggage. I was crying. I'd lost my little milk jug, which I was never without. My mother held us close to her so we wouldn't be lost in the commotion. I clutched at her *pagne*. We had to climb into the trucks, and quickly. We were crammed in like goats, all pressed together. We had to leave at once.

The trucks started off. A crowd had gathered by the side of the road to watch the convoy go past. Everyone was shouting, "There go the Tutsis," and they spat at us, waving machetes.

At first, I wasn't unhappy: a trip in a car was a novelty for me. But the journey turned more and more unpleasant: it went on forever, we were so tightly packed in, we crashed together with every bump in the road, we had to struggle not to suffocate, we were thirsty, there was no water. The children were crying. Whenever we drove by a river or lake, the men beat on the roof of the driver's cab to ask him to stop. But the trucks kept on going. Night had fallen. No one knew where we were headed. I saw despair in my mother's eyes. I was afraid.

1960: Internal exile

I don't know how long the trip lasted. Much later, I learned that the convoy had traveled through Burundi: Ngozi, Kirundo. Finally the trucks stopped in a schoolyard. We were surprised by the heat. We'd started off in Butare, in the mountains, where the weather's always cool. Everyone was desperately thirsty. The women were nursing already-weaned children so they'd have something to drink. The men went off to look for water. We truly were in an unknown land, nothing like Rwanda.

I don't know when my parents realized they'd been deported to Nyamata, in the district called Bugesera. Bugesera! To every Rwandan, there was something sinister in that name. It was an almost unpopulated savannah, home to big wild animals, infested by tsetse flies. They said the king sent disgraced chiefs into exile there.

We also soon saw that we weren't the first Tutsis to be displaced to Nyamata. Others were already there, people from the North, especially Ruhengeri. They'd been placed around the village of Nyamata proper and north of there, toward the valley of the Nyabarongo, in Kanzenze, in Kibungo. We southerners were the last to arrive. There were a few families from Gitarama and Gikongoro provinces in our convoy, but most of them were from Butare. At first they crowded us into the empty primary school classrooms. As the days went by, the women set up their kitchens in the schoolyard, simple shelters made with four stakes and a straw roof – *ibikoni*. The children went looking for the three big stones that traditionally form the hearth. There was no rain. This was the dry season, probably the summer of 1960. What I remember is the soldiers. They were housed in the schoolyard too, in sheet-metal huts. They sat there all day long, doing nothing, probably keeping an eye on us, their rifles between their legs. We thought they were very black. We called them the Congolese. We children weren't afraid of them. They gave us cookies, they always had cookies to give us. We spent our time sitting next to them so they'd give us cookies – *ibisuguti*. But they didn't speak our language. We didn't talk with them. They gave us cookies, and that's all.

Facing the school we'd been housed in, at the other end of the courtyard from the women's makeshift kitchens, stood an old colonial building with high white walls. We called it Tripolo's house, maybe from the nickname given to a Belgian administrator. The food they gave out to us was stored inside.

One evening, not long after we arrived, while the women were busy making the meal, while my mother, whose side I never left, was trying to shoo me away for fear I might be burned, we saw gigantic shadows appear on the big white wall of Tripolo's house, and those shadows spoke and they looked like people. Everyone stood glued to the spot, fascinated by those images, which seemed to be alive on the white wall, speaking words we understood. It was in Kirundi, but we understood. There was a mother and her child. And the child said, *"Umutsima uratakaye ma* – I knocked my paste over, Mama." And the mother answered, *"Hora ndawucumbe ndaguha undi* – It doesn't matter, I'll make another batch and give you some more." That was the only scene I can remember from the only movie I ever saw in Rwanda. For a few days, when night fell, we sat down in front of the big white wall and waited for the moving pictures to come back, but the mysterious projectionist never returned.

At first, it was the soldiers who distributed the food. Every morning the refugees would line up for their *pocho*, their ration. That job fell to the men. Not even widows went to pick up their rations. They always found some kindly soul to go in their place. But these distributions didn't go well. The soldiers hurried the line along with blows from their rifle butts. There were scuffles and shouts. The Tutsis prized their dignity above all. They couldn't tolerate humiliation and disorder. A delegation of important men, my father among them, negotiated an agreement by which the refugees themselves would hand out the rations, and from then on everything went smoothly.

The food they gave us seemed very strange. There was a white powder you were supposed to dissolve in water, and we were expected to drink that nameless liquid. It surely wasn't milk, because it didn't come from a cow, and besides, tradition dictates that milk is drunk not from metal containers but from jugs carved from the wood of certain trees, and treated with deep respect. The adults indignantly refused to drink, but the children were dying of hunger, so the mothers had a taste and then gave that powdered milk to the children.

Then there were the tomatoes. We were familiar with tomatoes, of course, but little ones, cherry-sized, used for making sauce and cooking bananas. The tomatoes they gave us were huge. We didn't know what to do with them. My parents refused to eat them raw. But since there was nothing else, they forced them on the children. I wept as I ate my first tomatoes.

——— ——— ———

Nyamata's displaced people hoped they would be able to go home once the troubles were over. The families had abandoned the class-rooms and built huts in the courtyard and around the school. There was no lack of grass in the savannah. But everything was meant to be temporary; there was no question of settling here. We would go home again very soon, back to Rwanda, because nobody thought of Nyamata as Rwanda.

Early one morning, trucks came rolling in again. They had us gather in the schoolyard. Everyone was thinking, "They've come for us at last, now the exile is over, we're going home." They did a roll call, all this for the sake of a few Hutu families who'd been taken away by mistake. They would be going "back to Rwanda," as we said. Among them was the family of Yosefu, whose wife Nyirabasesa was a Hutu. They were friends of ours: Nyirabasesa and my mother liked to confer on what to do with the yellow flour and other unknown ingredients we were given. I played with the children. We ate together. They went away in almost empty trucks.

Despair fell over everyone left behind. They understood: they would never go home again. Because they were Tutsis, they were condemned to live like pariahs or plague-carriers, on a reservation with no hope of escape. But that despair was the cement of a solidarity far stronger than any supposed ethnic spirit had ever created. The huts I mentioned earlier were built by the whole community, in order of need. Since my mother was pregnant, my family was among the first to move out of the classroom. Latrines were dug. Water-fetching duties were assigned. The governing committee appointed Rugereka, the son of the sculptor Kagango, to keep order at Rwakibirizi spring. Rugereka was a very young man, with a remarkable hairstyle imitated by all the other young men, even my brother Antoine. I don't know if it was his beautiful hair that allowed him to impose his authority, but in any case everyone quietly waited their turn to fill up the few containers we'd been given on our arrival.

We children, and there were many of us, wandered like lost souls in search of somewhere to play. The schoolyard was taken up by the families' huts and the soldiers' camp: no room to play with the balls and marbles the boys made from old sacks once used for flour or powdered milk, and no room for the girls' hopscotch course either. For that reason we wandered off into the wilderness, where it was tempting to taste the unknown fruit the bushes seemed to be offering us. "Whatever you do, don't touch those," our parents were forever warning us, "they're poison!" We looked longingly at the bushes and their forbidden fruit, but we never dared touch them.

And so opening a school was an urgent priority. There was no point hoping for anything from the authorities, but the schoolteachers among the displaced got help from the missionaries and set up classrooms under the trees. They even managed to administer the national exam that lets some students go on to secondary school. My brother André passed. He went off to middle school in Zaza, in the east, near the border with what is now Tanzania. Despite my fierce opposition, my father enrolled me in primary school. I found one thing to like about that: for lunch they gave us rice, furnished by the mission. In enormous pots, Rutabana did the cooking for the school: generously salted rice with milk. Needless to say, the rice stuck to the bottom of the pot and tasted burned. But for me, Rutabana's rice was the best, much better than the rice that was very occasionally included in our rations and cooked by my mother.

It was in fact precisely for the sake of that rice that my father had sent me to school despite my young age. The authorities and the priests were pressuring us to go off and settle into villages that they claimed had been built specially for us. No one would move. Leaving our temporary camp meant accepting our terrible fate, giving up on going back to Rwanda, on going home, and no one wanted any part of that. But soon there was no choice: in hopes of forcing us out, they cancelled the daily rations – the only food we had. Only children enrolled in the schools still got rice from the mission. Every family was given a machete for clearing brush, a mattock for working the soil, some seeds, and found themselves, sick at heart, assigned to one of those bush villages we were assured would be waiting for us to move in. The one we were sent to was called Gitwe.

Bugesera: Surviving in the bush

Gitwe was a very straight dirt road through the brush, leading nowhere. On either side of that long strip of red clay, in spaces more or less cleared but for the most part taken over by brambles, a number of little sheds had been built, sheet-metal roof resting on wooden beams, with no walls or rooms. What were those shelters there for? I've always wondered. Were they meant for us, or was this one of those agricultural settlement projects so dear to the hearts of the colonial authorities? I suspect the latter. Some hitch must have made them give up on the project, or else there weren't enough volunteer immigrants. Displaced by force, the Tutsis were there to be used, perfect guinea pigs who didn't have to give their consent.

Dropped like so many Robinson Crusoes into the middle of the savannah, the families had to put walls on the houses, clear the thick brush for their plantings, and find some way to feed themselves while they awaited the first harvest. The tradition in Rwanda is that all the neighbors lend a hand with the work. To repay them, the person being helped passes around generous jugs of sorghum beer, and the hard work ends in dancing and songs. In Gitwe, though, no one was in the mood to make beer, and it was impossible anyway. Like it or not, everyone had to try to get by on their own. But everyone was convinced Gitwe was a temporary encampment: one day or another, we'd go home again, we would go back to Rwanda.

Each family divided up the work among themselves. The men – which in our case meant my father and my big brother Antoine – saw to making the house livable and to clearing the field for our crops. Until that presumed harvest came, it was up to the women to somehow feed the family.

It very soon became clear that the only way to get hold of a little food was to go and work for the locals, the Bagesera. While Alexia stayed home to do the housekeeping, my mother went off every morning at first light, with my little sister Julienne on her back and me following after, clinging to her *pagne*. The area was sparsely populated, the houses widely scattered, and since it was all new to us we didn't know which way to set off at first. We climbed to the top of a hill to look for smoke, the sign of an enclosure. Then we set off across the savannah, listening intently for noises from the bush. We held our breath. It wasn't so much the elephants or the leopards that frightened us. It was the buffalo. "A buffalo never gives you warning," my mother said. "It just charges."

The Bagesera were welcoming, but they were poor. Many of them were worn down by sleeping sickness. Very few had anything to spare. Those who agreed to hire us gave us a few sweet potatoes for a day's work; you could get a little bunch of bananas if you spent two days working in the fields with no payment the first day. But we were living from hand to mouth, and my mother couldn't take the risk of going home with nothing, so most often she settled for sweet potatoes.

As I remember, we often worked for one particular family who proved especially hospitable. The mother's name was Kabihogo. I've forgotten the father's. They only had one child, a girl near my age, so they were happy for the help. While my mother worked in the fields, I swept the yard. The little girl wanted to play with me. That gave me an excuse for a break. Sometimes they even let me eat with her. In the evening we went home with a little basket of sweet potatoes. Kabihogo had taken to me, and often she set a few aside just for me, carefully packed in straw – the best ones, *gahungezi*, with bright red skin but very white flesh. Back home, I was proud to show my brother Antoine and my sisters how much I'd earned in a day.

As I say, Bugesera was a backwater. There weren't many schools, and although there was a mission at Nyamata, Christianity never took hold, so the traditional rites were still widely practiced. One morning my mother, who was raised by nuns with a horror of what they called "pagan superstitions," came face-to-face with one of those rites.

We were paid by the chore, so we always got to the house of someone with work for us as early as we could. One morning, in an enclosure we often went to – Sakagabo's house – no one answered the call we shouted out, as politeness requires, before we entered the yard. Everything was silent, and we were wondering what had become of them when all at once we heard a commotion in the banana grove. A crowd appeared through the trees, men and women completely naked, their faces rubbed with white dirt. Beneath those frightening masks, I hardly recognized the family we often worked for. But it was them – the father, the mother, the children – along with others I didn't know, maybe neighbors. My mother immediately made the sign of the cross, took me by the hand, and off we ran. We hurried through the brush, never turning around. My mother didn't say a word. She was running like a madwoman. Once we were home, she washed me with all the medicinal plants she could gather, invoking the Virgin Mary all the while. We had to be purified, as did everything that might have come into contact with those people who celebrated the Kubandwa cult, who were Imandwa, possessed by evil spirits whose chief was the devil himself, Ryangombe! She was sure it would bring us misfortune, that everything they'd given us to eat was the food of the devil. Five years old, I looked uncomprehendingly at my mother as she trembled in terror of beliefs that were the beliefs of her parents.

The men had a terrible time clearing the brush and digging out the roots; the stubborn brambles resisted the machetes we'd been given, our only tools. To protect themselves from the thorns, they'd made themselves crude, oversize sandals from old tires they'd picked up at the mission. As soon as a patch of land was cleared, my father randomly sowed all the seeds he'd been given in Nyamata. The soil had never been farmed, and at first it was very fertile: soon we saw carrots coming up, but also lettuce and radishes, which we immediately pulled out, thinking they must be weeds. The carrots were particularly plentiful. My father roasted them in a big fire in the middle of the field and forced us to eat them, despite our mistrust of alien vegetables. He himself wouldn't touch them, for the sake of his dignity.

My mother was impatient for the "real" harvest to come: the sorghum harvest. When it did, we gathered only the heads, dried them, and beat them with a big spatula – an *umwuko* – to loosen the seeds, which we sieved and crushed with the grinding stone. Every evening my mother made sorghum paste with the flour. That was the only food that really filled you up, she thought. I hated sorghum paste, so I always made sure to sit in the shadows, far from the fire, where I could discreetly slip the balls of sorghum through the holes and cracks in the hut's clay wall. My parents would find them the next morning, at the base of the wall. It wasn't hard to collar the culprit.

You don't sleep well on an empty stomach. I spent much of the night moaning and waking my mother: I was afraid I might die of hunger. It's also true that the makeshift beds we used in our early days at Gitwe were not exactly conducive to restful sleep. We'd had neither the time nor the means to weave the mats Rwandans use as bedding. We lay down right on the straw, which was soon infested with bedbugs and chigoe fleas. Changing the straw did no good: the parasites were still there. Sometimes we also came under attack from a column of ants attracted by a scrap of food. I was always relieved to hear my mother's footsteps, which meant that the fears and torments of the night would soon be at an end.

———— ———— ————

One of the greatest difficulties the refugees in Gitwe faced was water. Rwanda is a high-altitude country, somewhere around 6500 feet, so there's plenty of rainfall, but it's different in Bugesera: as the geography textbooks say, it's a dry savannah, at medium altitude (4000 to 4250 feet) – little rain, and even fewer sources of water. The main spring is close to Nyamata. Its name is Rwakibirizi. Tradition says that it sprang up under the spear of Ruganzu Ndori, one of the heroic founders of Rwanda, so he could give water to his dogs, which were dying of thirst. But Rwakibirizi was a long way from Gitwe. It took a full day to go there and fetch water. That was my brother Antoine's job. He would come back with a two-day supply in jugs we'd got from the Batwa in exchange for a few sweet potatoes – a temporary solution, because soon our gourd plants would give us calabashes to use. We also tried to save up the water from the occasional rainfall, with gutters built from pieces of sheet metal gathered in the village of Nyamata. We also went off to search for puddles that might still be left at the bottom of a valley or in the hollow of a rock, an *ibinamba*. But those quickly dried up. There was a spring closer to Gitwe, but it gave only a tiny trickle. It took time to fill a calabash, so there was always someone there fetching water and others waiting their turn. Antoine preferred to go in the middle of the night, not wanting to waste the daylight hours, and hoping he'd find no one there. My mother wanted me to go with him. She was afraid he might fall asleep from exhaustion by the spring and be eaten by a wild animal. I stayed close by his side, refusing to hear the rustlings, the howls, the sound of galloping hooves from the bush.

Living in Gitwe, maybe even more than in the rest of Bugesera, meant living on the turf of big, wild animals. The lions and buffalo soon left us in peace, but the elephants were drawn to the banana grove as soon as it was planted, and they feasted all night long. The leopards were forever prowling among the houses. They were like cats: every family had its own. It would come inside in the night.

Lying in the bed we shared, Julienne and I could hear it rattling the piece of sheet metal that served as our front door. We knew it was there: we lay waiting for the rustling sound that meant it was close by. My father had put up partitions to separate the children from the parents' room. We slept in the communal room, where the hearth was, where cooking was done, where the family gathered in the evening. Before everyone went to bed, a few embers were pushed under the ash, and logs piled on top to get the fire going the next morning. Suddenly we heard the pile of wood collapsing. Looking out through the holes in the mat that served as our blanket, we saw the leopard's eyes, even brighter than the flying sparks, and our blood ran cold. Julienne and I lay there completely still. Mama had told us not to move, no matter what. "If you do," she would say, "he'll think you're showing a lack of respect."

We both lay stock-still under the mat, waiting for daybreak to come so we could be sure that our leopard had gone on its way. Every evening, at nightfall, we trembled as we waited for its next visit.

The Bagesera were great hunters, of course. Often we heard the sound of their trumpets, big antelope horns – *ihembe* – announcing that the hunt had begun. Armed only with bows and spears, they hunted even the rogue elephants that demolished their crops, but they didn't eat them. The hyenas and vultures went after the massive carcasses as they rotted in the bush. When we went to work in their fields, the Bagesera would tell us, "Watch out for the *ubushya*!" We soon discovered what an *ubushya* was: a trap, a big trench that they dug around their fields for protection. The trenches were covered over with grass, and the animals fell into them. We dug *ubushya* of our own wherever we found animals often passed by, thanks to which we could get meat for ourselves. No one minded eating antelope or gazelle: evidently they tasted like beef. But the men adamantly refused to touch warthog.

When we first came to Gitwe, there was no school. Then, after a few months, the refugees managed to put together a class. Again the mission agreed to provide rice. Rutabana went back to his huge cookpots. I rediscovered the rice I so loved, and this time I was actually old enough to go to school. Classes were held under tall trees we called *iminazi*. They bore beautiful fruits, like apricots, that fell on us as we sat. We ate them as our teacher, Bukuba, taught the lesson.

There were a few Bagesera among the pupils, and they taught us a great deal. They introduced the little refugees to all the wealth of the savannah. And the bush was filled with all sorts of fruit! There were *imisagara*, which looked like sorghum seeds, slightly bitter but easy to gather, even for the tiniest children. The *iminyonza* were also within everyone's reach, but you had to watch out for thorns. Gathering *amasarazi* and *amabungo* was harder. You had to climb the trees. We worked in teams. Some climbed the trees, others stood underneath to pick up the fruit, and also to chase away larcenous monkeys or rival gatherers. I myself didn't want to climb. It was my friend Candida, a real tomboy, who scrambled up to the top. We loved *amabungo* most of all. It was a vine that climbed along the trunks of the tall trees. You could find that fruit only where the brush was particularly dense, far from the houses, on the heights, at Gisunzu. It was a veritable expedition, and you had to choose: go to school or gather *amabungo*. Very often we chose *amabungo*.

So that we would be forgiven, Candida and I brought back *amabungo* for the whole family. Our harvests were awaited at home like so many rare treats. Only my father couldn't bring himself to taste the wild delicacies of the bush.

——— ——— ———

Once we'd more or less assured our survival, we considered how to go about earning some money. We had to buy salt. We had to buy fabric for our clothes, because the few *pagnes* we'd been wearing since Magi were now falling into rags. Above all, we needed money to pay Alexia's and André's tuition. My father went looking for work. He knew how to keep books – a rare and valuable skill. He was hired in an infirmary in Ngenda, a long way from Gitwe. We only saw him on Sundays. Nothing defeated my father. Even with all the trouble that had come crashing down on us, he never gave up. Not only did he work in Ngenda, he also thought nothing of walking all the way to Kigali if he glimpsed some possibility of earning money for Alexia's and André's studies. As he walked, he went days without eating and sometimes nights without sleeping, because he took advantage of the cool after sunset to cover as much ground as he could. He ended up with tuberculosis and was hospitalized for months in the sanatorium at Gishari. But he never abandoned what had become for him his life's single goal: making it possible for his children to go to school.

Ever industrious, my mother began to grow peanuts between the dirt road and the house. I went off to sell them at the market in Nyamata. She set aside two little plots for Alexia and me to farm on our own. Alas! Our gardens were soon taken away from us. Even in the depths of the bush, "civilization" was catching up with us. They (who "they" were, I have no idea) made a rule that every family had to grow coffee plants. By all appearances, "they" hadn't given up on the old colonial farming projects. Every family had to grow a certain number of plants, and they had to be planted along the dirt road, in front of the house, so they'd be easier to inspect and eventually to harvest. We had to pull out all our own plantings, and even worse, uproot a good part of the banana grove, which was just beginning to bear fruit. We had to go all the way to Rwakibirizi, more than ten kilometers from Gitwe, to pick up the plants. Coffee plants take a great deal of care, and they left us little time to tend our field. School was no longer the children's priority: our first job was to change the mulch around the coffee plants. Whenever the grown-ups turned their backs, we seized the opportunity to lie down for a few minutes on that mat of fine grasses, because it was much softer than our beds. But those breaks never lasted long. The agronomists sent to teach us how to grow coffee kept a close eye on us. They came from the Karama Agricultural Institute. With our bare feet, we were fascinated by the polished black leather of their boots.

1961-1964:
"Democratic" exclusion

On July 1, 1962, Rwanda officially became independent. With the aid of the Belgians and the Catholic church, the MDR-Parmehutu could establish what a UN report from March 1961 called a "single-party racial dictatorship." Thousands of Tutsis had been massacred, more than one hundred fifty thousand had fled to neighboring countries, and those who stayed behind in Rwanda would be forced to live as outcasts. In Nyamata, the internal refugees were subjected to the benefits of ethnic *demokarasi*.

My father had a bitter memory of that democracy's inauguration. The history books say it came on September 25th, 1961, the day of the legislative elections. They didn't skimp on the democracy in

Nyamata. They'd built little straw cabins for voting booths; facing them, in the open air, was a big table and a box. Excited by the novelty, the children played around the little cabins. My father and other refugees he'd convinced to come out and vote presented themselves at the big table that served as a polling station. Piles of ballots were very visibly laid out, one pile for each party. But, on either side of the table, the town councillor Mbarubukeye and his men stood looking on with a threatening air, and another councillor, Bwanakumi, was sitting behind the table. Bwanakumi handed out the ballot and envelopes, and patiently watched as each voter put the ballots in the envelope and the envelope in the box, before the vigilant eyes and the ever-more menacing truncheons of Mbarubukeye and his gang. And that, said my father, was how he and all the Tutsi refugees in Nyamata ended up voting for Kayibanda, who'd vowed to destroy us.

The refugees did their best to convince themselves that they would one day go home (and those who stored up reserves or plowed new land for their fields were mocked), but despair often got the better of them, and sinister rumors of the fate that awaited us made the rounds. There was talk of the Rwabayanga, the bottomless pits. These were three very deep crevasses on the Burundi border. The plan had been to throw the Tutsis into them when they first got here in 1960. Why that had never happened no one knew. The Bagesera were the first to speak of them. Then my brother Antoine's friend Froduald had seen them. He worked in the tsetse eradication campaign, traveling all over the region, even as far away as Kirundo, in Burundi. He too had seen the crevasses one day, but, he said with a laugh, "there are a lot more dead elephants in there than dead Tutsis." Nonetheless, people went on talking about the Rwabayanga, and whenever someone disappeared, which happened often, they said he'd been thrown into the Rwabayanga.

——— ——— ———

In late 1963, a rumor spread through Nyamata: King Kigeli was going to return and lead the displaced people back home. The rumor's source in Gitwe was our neighbor Sebeza. His oldest son Kazubwenge had left for Burundi, but his parents had heard he would soon be coming back, and he wouldn't be alone. He would be with the king, who was returning to lead the downtrodden deportees home again.

Everyone made feverish preparations for the king's arrival and our return to Rwanda. The men constructed oversize bows in honor of the eagerly awaited sovereign. They weren't war weapons, and no one had any intention of using them. They were only meant to show the king that they'd stayed faithful to him, that they were still his men, his *ingabo* – his warriors. My father made a particularly big bow, the biggest in the village. It was hung up over the hearth, not too visibly, wrapped in a fine mat called an *ikirago*, because deep down no one was entirely convinced that the king would be coming to take us away. As for the women, they made *urugori*, crowns of sorghum bark that mothers wear as a sign of fertility and the permanence of the family. They'd chosen the widest pieces of bark, which turned a beautiful golden color as they dried, and they'd inscribed the words "Long live Kigeli!" with a metal point heated in the fire. This was all done in secret, of course, but with the utmost excitement.

And then one fine day – it would have been somewhere around Christmas, if we can believe the historians – everyone emerged from their houses well before dawn, dressed in their finest clothes, as if for Mass. All the mamas had carefully shaved their children's heads, leaving nothing but one pretty, round tuft of hair, the *igisage*, on the front of the skull. No one went off to their field. The men stood in the middle of the road, with a serious air, speaking in turns. The women went off and sat down on the termite mound they used as a meeting place. We children danced around it; we didn't know quite why we were dancing, but we danced. It seems to me that the sun rose earlier than usual. The great day had come, our long-awaited deliverance was at hand.

Slowly the hours went by. Morning came to an end. The women went off to feed their children. Nothing was happening. Everyone listened for some sound. The men had fallen silent. Finally, we heard a distant rumble, growing slowly louder. That noise didn't fill us with confidence. It wasn't the cheers we'd been expecting, the cries of triumph. And then all at once we saw black dots appear in the sky, black dots speeding straight for us. We'd heard of helicopters, but we'd never seen one: the *ngombabishire*, the exterminators! Now they were almost overhead. Terrified, everyone began to run. The fastest ones took cover in the bush, while others, more fear-crazed or less vigorous – the children above all – burrowed under the thick straw mulch around the new coffee plants, but the helicopters flew back and forth above us, just off the ground, kicking up the straw and uncovering anyone trying to hide under the last remaining stalks.

I don't know how I ended up under a bush at the far end of the field with my little sister Julienne. The helicopters went back and forth over the houses. My parents and big brother had disappeared. I never found out where they'd hidden, maybe on Rebero Hill, where, some thirty years later, the last surviving inhabitants of Gitwe and Gitagata would resist to the end the attacks of the murderers trying to finish their "work."

The helicopters went away, but soon we saw a long row of trucks coming toward us. The trucks were filled with soldiers firing in every direction and throwing grenades. They jumped down from the trucks, searched the banana groves, pillaged the houses. But evidently they didn't dare venture into the bush, where we were hiding. When night came they got back in their trucks and drove off.

My little sister and I stayed hidden in our thicket all night long. Desperately hungry, we crawled to the very end of the field and dug up a few sweet potatoes. We ate them raw, then hurried back to the shelter of the bush, our hearts pounding. Everything was strangely silent. Even the animals seemed to be keeping quiet. A little before dawn, we saw the neighbor's son Kazubwenge coming home, looking worn and exhausted, his clothes in rags. There were three or four other young men with him, men I didn't know, armed only with bows. They crept around, from one house to the next, then went off in the dim, early-morning light. I think I heard them say, "It's all over, there's no hope." I don't know if I really heard them say that.

——— ——— ———

Over the next few days, the refugees gradually returned to their houses. The men hurried to break their beautiful bows, and the women tore up their sorghum-bark crowns.

They could hardly bear to do it, knowing the bad luck it would bring them. And indeed, the soldiers came back, patrolling all through the area, in the houses, in the bush. Now they weren't afraid. They were emboldened. They wore their helmets pulled down low on their heads. We thought we could see implacable hatred in their eyes. They called us *Inyenzi* – cockroaches. From now on, in Nyamata, we would all be Inyenzi. I was an Inyenzi.

The soldiers arrested many people, starting with teachers and shopkeepers with businesses in Nyamata's little town center. Among them were Bwankoko – his daughter Marie was in my class – and Ruboneka, whose wife Scholastique was so kind: when the teacher sent us home from school because he thought our heads were badly shaved, we ran straight to Scholastique, who was always ready to be our *coiffeuse*. Bwankoko, Ruboneka, and many more were taken off to the prison in Ruhengeri. They never came back.

One shopkeeper had a business in Nyamata like the others, but lived in Gitwe. His name was Tito, and he came from Butare. The soldiers showed up to take him away. Through our sheet-metal doors, we heard the sound of boots, the clamor of rifle butts hitting Tito's door. We heard the sobs of his wife Felicita, the cries of his children. People who'd ventured outside told us the soldiers had searched and sacked the house like all the others, but they'd also dragged Tito away to their truck. His son Apollinaire, who must have been four years old, ran up and clung to his father. Felicita shouted to him to let go and come back to her. But Apollinaire wouldn't listen: he kept his little arms wrapped around his father's legs. Then the soldier said – and the whole village heard – "Well, if he wants to go with his father, let's take him too. After all, he's the son of an Inyenzi, he's a baby snake, a baby cockroach. One day he'll be a big snake himself, a real cockroach, an Inyenzi." The soldiers threw Tito and his son into the truck, and we never saw them again.

A suicidal offensive launched from Burundi by a hundred-some badly armed refugees gave the government of Grégoire Kayibanda a pretext to initiate a brutal repression of all Tutsis still living in the country. The months of January and February 1964 were a real foretaste of the 1994 genocide. They were especially bloody in Gikongoro province. My parents sometimes spoke of family members who'd stayed behind in Cyanika, whom they never saw again. My mother had heard that the Rukarara ran red with blood. One day Karozeti, a little boy of five or six, appeared in the village. He was the nephew of Bukuba, the schoolteacher. He'd come from Gikongoro. His whole family had been massacred. He was the only survivor. No one knew how he'd found his way to Nyamata. The phrase "unaccompanied minor" hadn't been invented yet.

Bertrand Russell was all alone when he condemned "the most horrible and systematic human massacre we have had occasion to witness since the extermination of the Jews by the Nazis." The Catholic church, the former mandate authority, the international criminal courts, none of them had anything to say, apart from denouncing Inyenzi terrorism.

Hundreds of thousands of Tutsis chose exile. Many of the families in Nyamata left for Burundi. It wasn't hard: the border was close by, and you could make a discreet escape through the thick, uninhabited bush. But soon a great influx of soldiers arrived at Gako military camp. From now on, the displaced people of Nyamata would be under heavy surveillance. Maybe the soldiers had been sent to prevent a mass escape, maybe to fight off potential incursions; more than anything, they were there to impose a daily regime of terror on every last refugee.

Gitagata: The fields, the school, the parish

As I just said, a good number of Nyamata's displaced people fled to Burundi. Many of the lots had no one living on them. That was when my father decided we should move. After a few good harvests, Gitwe's soil was depleted, and turned out not to be very fertile. People said the harvests were better near Lake Cyohoha – Lake Cyohoha North, that is – so we set off down the road for Gitagata. We moved into an abandoned house, formerly lived in by Mbayiha, an energetic young man who'd managed to clear a sizable patch of land. My father declared it just right for our family. He thrust his stick into the ground. The ground of Gitagata. He would spend the rest of his life there. He would be killed there, along with my mother. Nothing remains of all that now. The killers attacked the house until every last trace was wiped away. The bush has covered everything over. It's as if we never existed. And yet my family once lived there. Humiliated, afraid, waiting day after day for what was to come, what we didn't have a word for: genocide. And I alone preserve the memory of it. That's why I'm writing this.

That move was another heartbreak for my mother, like a second exile. In Gitwe, families from Gikongoro and Butare were placed together. My mother had her friends right on her doorstep, so to speak. In spite of everything, we still felt somewhat at home there, which at least helped us bear the burden of our sadness. In Gitagata, on the other hand, most of the displaced came from Ruhengeri, from the North, strangers to us southerners. We'd have to find some way to earn their acceptance, and get used to seeing our friends only on Sundays, after Mass. My mother dreaded that, but she faced the prospect with her usual courage, and never let anything show.

Those days in Gitagata! The days of my childhood! So many were days of pain and sadness . . . And then others were strangely peaceful, as if our tormentors had forgotten us. Ordinary childhood days, few and far between.

Days in Gitagata began before dawn. My mother was always the first one up. She washed her feet in the fresh dew and then went to knock on the neighbors' doors. She was the one who woke up the whole village. Meanwhile, my father pulled away the mats we used as blankets, shouting *"Henuka! Henuka!* Get up!" And we jumped out of bed.

There was much to be done before we went off to school: fetch water, sweep the house and the yard. Alexia and I shared the chores. In the early days, we also shared my mother's *pagne*: it was the only one we had in the house. Then my mother, who knew how to sew, made us a dress – but Alexia and I still only had one dress between us. And so one day it was Alexia who went to school with the dress, and the next day it was me. I happily gave up my turn with it, because I vastly preferred staying home with my mother. Meanwhile, my father had tied on his little white *pagne*: he was off to Mass. He went to Mass every day.

My mother always set aside a few sweet potatoes for my lunch; she wrapped them up in banana leaves, and I ran off. Starting from the third year of primary school, we went to the big school in Nyamata. I ran all the way there. As I ran, I said hello to the women sweeping the little paths in front of their houses. As I ran, I called out to my friends to see if they'd already set off. Candida would be waiting for me beside the dirt road. I ran all the way to the school, put my little cache of sweet potatoes at the back of the classroom, and hurried around behind the school buildings where the girls were playing hopscotch. The boys had taken over the playground, juggling a banana-leaf soccer ball with their feet. That was off-limits to us.

The start to the schoolday seemed to me a grandiose and elaborate ceremony. The drumbeat sounded. All the pupils gathered on the playground in neat rows, by class. We sang the national anthem as the flag was raised. The drum sounded again, and we all headed off toward our classrooms and lined up, the smallest ones in front, the bigger ones behind, one line of boys, one line of girls. The teacher stood watching over us from the doorway, his stick behind his back. The drum gave the signal to enter the classrooms. We stayed on our feet as the teacher walked through the room, stick in hand. In chorus, we called out: "Good morning, teacher!" Once he reached the blackboard, he signaled his pet to say the prayer, and the whole class prayed along. At last we could sit down, and the lessons began. Woe unto any straggler who still dared to come in – the teacher's stick recognized no excuse!

There was one excuse, though, that was accepted by teachers and parents alike: an encounter with elephants. Elephants often walked through the villages on their way from one remaining patch of wilderness to another. Sometimes, it's not clear why, one of them followed the road. Our parents had told us: "Whatever you do, stay behind the elephant, never pass him, never get in front of him." We thus followed behind as the animal majestically walked along, as if out for a stroll. Rwandans have always admired the elephant's walk, which they consider graceful and elegant; when women dance, they're paying homage to the noble pachyderm. We scrupulously followed our parents' instructions, keeping our distance from the animal, imitating its pauses and detours. Sometimes a whole morning went by before the elephants decided to turn away. There was no point going to school now; better to go looking for *amabungo* to pick. We knew our parents wouldn't say anything, since we'd been following an elephant.

Still, elephants weren't the greatest danger schoolchildren could meet with on the road to Nyamata. There was also the cruelty of men . . . But I'll save that for later.

Later, too, we saw the elephants again. They were on trucks. I think they were being moved to Akagera National Park.

It was at school that I learned there were other books than the Bible. My father's Bible was the only book we had in our house. Every morning he laid it on the shelf that should have been taken up by milk jugs, a household's most precious possession – but we had no cows, and so no milk. Next to the Bible sat a bottle of Benedictine, empty of course. That was also an object to be treated with reverence. My father said Benedictine was the drink of the king. The king drank the white people's nectar. I secretly thought that might have brought him misfortune. But my father was proud of his bottle.

At school, the teacher had a neat stack of books on his desk, and sometimes he handed them out, one for every two or three of us. The book was called *African Mornings*. But the Africa we read about there wasn't our Africa. Not the Africa where Rwanda was, at least. There were so many strange things: baobabs, oxbow lakes . . . The children were named Mamadou, Fatoumata. "Fatoumata?" we would say. "There's no such thing as Fatoumata, it's Fortunata. That's a real girl's name." That would make the teacher angry: "Fatoumata!" he would say. "Repeat after me: Fatoumata!" And, although we still had our doubts, we repeated after him: "Fatoumata! Fatoumata!" Nonetheless, thanks to that book, we sensed that the world was far bigger than we could imagine. And there were such wonderful stories: Sinbad the sailor, Hiawatha and the wild ducks, Monsieur Seguin and his goat, the tortoise and the hare . . . Sometimes I dreamed of an impossible thing: having a book all to myself.

Of course, our work wasn't done when school let out. You might even say it was only beginning. Often, if we hadn't had a chance to go to the lake in the morning, we had to stop by the Rwakibirizi spring to draw water, and then as soon as we got home we had to hurry off and join our parents, who worked in the fields until nightfall. For the girls, there was also the cooking to do, and when the moon was full we swept the yard to save time the next morning.

But those jobs weren't always a chore. When there was no school, we set out in a group to do the washing on the shores of Lake Cyohoha. The lakeshore became a meeting place for all the local girls. We went in the hottest hours of the day, when no one came to fetch water. We settled down on the shore, in the grass, which was always very green, like a lawn in a garden. We sorted the laundry, washed it in the lakewater, singing all the while, and then laid it out on the grass. While we were waiting for it to dry, we bathed, washed our hair. Some even tried to swim, but we never ventured into the papyrus, for fear of running into a crocodile. Then the hairdressing session began on the grass.

The laundry was soon dry, so we went off before people started coming again to fetch water. We folded the clothes and wrapped them in a *pagne*. The little band of girls set off again, carrying the bundled clothes on their heads.

Alas! the lakeshore, which was like a garden for our innocent games, soon became a place of the most horrible nightmares.

——— ——— ———

On Wednesday afternoons, to prepare for first communion or confirmation, we studied the catechism with Kenderesire, a spinster who lived with her mother not far from the mission. Now and then that lesson ended with clothes being given out, second-hand clothes that supposedly came from America. That always drew a crowd. I never understood how people knew about the free clothes when they hadn't been at the lesson. In any case, they came to the mission in droves on those days. The priest stood at the top of the front steps – Father Ligi, an Italian, with his white gown and his fat stomach, as fat as the bag full of clothes that he set down beside him. Everyone looked at the bag, ready to pounce. The father didn't make a move, he made us wait. Then, all of a sudden, he reached into the bag and flung out an armload of clothes, and everyone rushed forward. The fastest ones got hold of the clothes, but the stronger and more ruthless ones ripped them from their hands. Soon it was an out-and-out brawl, kicking up a cloud of red dust. Then the good father called for his serving boy: "Nyabugigira! Nyabugigira!" Nyabugigira came with a bucket of water and handed it to the priest, who threw it over us to break up the melee. On those days we usually came home with our ragged clothes dripping wet and caked with red mud, and we hadn't snagged even one of those coveted garments. Christian charity was not without its humiliations.

My father was a very pious man. Every evening he gathered the family around him for a group prayer. He picked up his glasses, given to him by the fathers – he was the only one in the village who wore them – and opened the Bible to read us a passage. I don't know how he chose his readings. Often we walked in circles around the banana grove to say the rosary or follow the way of the cross. Woe unto anyone who shirked these devotional exercises: the paternal stick quickly set him back on the straight and narrow.

My father was proud to be the local head of the Legion of Mary. He obviously had no idea that one of that movement's first leaders was Grégoire Kayibanda, who, with the support of Monsignor Perraudin, made of it the embryo of the future MDR-Parmehutu ethnic party.

Sunday Mass at the Nyamata mission was the great event of the week. There were three masses, and every family sent a few of their number to each one, leaving someone at home to chase off the monkeys, always lying in wait to ravage our fields. My father went to all three. That was his big day. We saved our most respectable clothes for Mass. My mother went to the first mass, because she was always up early, but also so that she could lend me the beautiful white blouse Judith had brought her from Kigali, a blouse that on me became a white dress, in which I went proudly off to Mass. The women and children sat on one side of the church, the men on the other. The priest said Mass in Latin. At the foot of the altar, the choir assembled by Casimir, the fourth-year teacher at the primary school, sang hymns, and the assembly sang along, but no one clapped their hands: back then, clapping or dancing was unthinkable in a church. Using enormous pictures, the priest explained all the terrible punishments that awaited sinners. I trembled at the sight of the flames of Hell, with a multitude of damned souls swarming in the middle like terrified ants. I counted up my sins. There was no end to them. After confession, I always had a feeling I'd forgotten one. The biggest one of all. I went back to the good father, repeated the litany of my faults. In the end, weary of my scruples, he forbade me to come back.

The soldiers demanded that President Kayibanda's portrait be hung in every house. The missionaries made sure the image of Mary was put up beside him. We lived our lives under the twin portraits of the President who'd vowed to exterminate us and Mary who was waiting for us in heaven.

——— ——— ———

But on some days there was no question of prayers and processions, even for my father. Those were the days when we made banana beer, *urwarwa*. Making *urwarwa* was a major undertaking, requiring a great deal of time and the participation of the whole family, and even the neighbors. Those were festival days.

As everyone knows, the bananas used to make *urwarwa* aren't left to ripen on the tree: they ripen in broad ditches dug in the banana grove. At the bottom of the ditch you make a bed of very dry banana leaves, which you then set on fire. Dry leaves, and nothing else: you don't want coals, only ashes. Once the leaves have burned and the hole is hot, but not too hot – the bananas aren't supposed to cook – it's lined with big green banana leaves, big enough to overlap the edges. Then, when the leaves have been carefully laid out and the temperature is just right, the hole is filled with bananas and the green leaves are folded over to make a hermetic seal. Then you cover the whole thing with dirt and tamp it down with the back of a shovel.

Now there's nothing to do but wait. Everyone is excited. The children can't keep still. They dance as they wait for the big day to come.

At dawn on the fourth day, my father says to me: "Mukasonga! Mukasonga! Go see if the bananas are ripe." I run fast as I can to the banana grove. I very gently scrape away the dirt covering the ditch, I carefully fold back the leaves, I delicately reach in, taking care not to crush the bananas, I feel one of them: it's ripe! Everyone has been waiting for the signal. There's no question of going to school now. We have to hurry off and fetch water, ask a neighbor to lend us the canoe-shaped trough we'll use to crush the bananas with the *ishinge* grass my little sisters have gone to pick. You then take the bananas from the ditch and load them into baskets. You go back and forth between the banana hole and the trough, which is set up beneath the banana trees closest to the house, since they provide the shade required for this work, which will go on all day. My father and mother peel the bananas and put them in the trough. Lost in his task, my father never sees the bananas discreetly dropped along the way, with my mother's complicity, which we promise ourselves to come back and eat later.

You don't fill the trough all the way to the rim, because then the foam might overflow. This is when you press out their juice, using the handfuls of grass. You kneel down before the trough, you press the bananas, the juice comes out, the foam – *urofuro* – rises. As it rises, the children are allowed to eat it. The parents say it's good for you. It makes you strong. My mother gives us each a calabash full of foam. We dig in, we get it all over our faces, in our eyes, in our hair. There's no point trying to hide from the neighbors that we're making *urwarwa*, they'll soon notice the children adorned with a makeup of red-tinged foam.

Now you have the juice – *umutobe indakamirwa*. Next it has to be strained. As much water as juice will be poured into the trough, over the bed of *ishinge* impregnated with crushed-banana concentrate. You strain it, you wring it out – *gukamura*. That's how you make good *urwarwa*. Some people cheat, of course, stretching the juice by putting in more water, but the recipe for good *urwarwa* is one jug of water for every jug of juice.

Nothing is wasted. The *ishinge* grasses that were used to press the bananas, now impregnated with juice, are dropped into a jug, and water is poured over them. This infusion is called *amaganura*, drunk mostly by women and children, as a sign of friendship. The ladies' straws will drain the jug to the bottom, leaving only a little swamp of *ishinge*, with mosquitoes and gnats floating on top.

The jugs full of *umutobe* are wrapped in green leaves and put back into the hole, which has been heated to the proper temperature. By way of yeast, a little juice made from grilled and ground sorghum has been added to the *umutobe*. You then have to wait for two days. At nightfall on the second day, my father says to me: "Mukasonga! Mukasonga! Take a straw and go see if it's fermented." I run to one of the jugs, stick the straw down into it, suck at it, taste the delicious flavor. My father cries: "Mukasonga liked what she tasted! It must be good. The *urwarwa* is ready!"

Then you have to strain it again and divide it up into smaller jugs, some of which will be sold, others drunk with the neighbors. All of this goes on by night, and the sight of the hurricane lanterns coming and going soon alerts the neighbors, who come running to offer their expert opinion on the results. Staggering from too much drink, my father is proud of his work: the best *urwarwa* in the village!

——— ——— ———

But the truly happy days, the only ones I knew in my childhood, were the ones I spent with my mother. I've always loved working at home and in the fields. That might be why I chose social work as my trade – so I could stay close to the earth, to the peasants. How could I have known then that I would be exercising that profession not in Rwanda but in France?

So my mother picked up her mattock, and I picked up mine. We each had our own mattock, a big one for my mother – *isuka* – and for me a little one, an *ifuni*, matched to my size. As we walked to the fields, just after sunup, my mother would tell stories. She told of the great King Ruganzu Ndori, his exile in the land of his paternal aunt, the traps laid by the aunt's husband, the disclosure of the secrets of the kingdom, his return to Rwanda. It was a long story, it went on and on. I drowsed a little on my feet; sometimes, in the distance, I thought I could see Ruganzu with his spear, Ruganzu Cyambaran-tama cyi'Rwanda, crossing over the hills dressed in his sheepskin. My mother had shown me his footprints: behind the church, Ruganzu's feet had left their mark in the rock – there was even a hollow made

———

by his dog's little bottom. My mother believed you could find traces of Ruganzu everywhere in Rwanda. All of a sudden, I snapped out of my half-sleep and said to Mama: "More! More!"

My mother told of the coming of the white people, in her own way. "Digidigi came along," she said, "and everyone died." My mother was an orphan. Her parents had died in an epidemic of *mugiga* – perhaps meningitis. She was raised by her brother. The nuns of a nearby mission took the orphans in; my mother never learned to read or write, she was only taught to pray. Around her, the world was crumbling. The white people had locked the king away in a stone house. They'd violated the secrets of the kingdom. Karinga, the royal drum, was hidden in the swamps with the *umwiru*, its keeper . . .

At home, my mother taught me what every Rwandan girl needs to know: how to braid mats, how to weave elegant geometric baskets, how to recognize medicinal plants, make decoctions. Thanks to her, I knew how to make the best beer, choose the cuttings that would produce the finest sweet potatoes . . .

My mother carefully – piously would be a better word – farmed the old plants. She gave them a patch of land to themselves, nearby the house. She planted almost forgotten varieties of beans – *ububenga*, *kajemunkangara* – and sweet potatoes – *gahungezi*, *nyirabusegenya* – and gourds – *imyungu*, *nyirankuba*. There was also eleusine, an ancient African cereal whose grains are like mustard seeds, and *inkori*, which is a sort of little lentil. Many of those seeds came from Magi: she'd saved them in the knot of her *pagne* like the most precious of all treasures. She was always looking for rare rootstocks on the Bagesera properties, and she did extra work so she could take them. Sometimes she spent a whole afternoon on the little patch of land she set aside for the plants no one grew anymore. For her they were like the survivors of a happier time, and she seemed to draw a new energy from them. She grew them not for daily consumption but as a way of bearing witness to what was in danger of disappearing, what did indeed disappear in the cataclysm of the genocide. When Mama cooked with them, I thought I was tasting the magical food people eat in stories.

Late in the evening, the time for storytelling, my mother once again picked up the tireless thread of her tales: "When I was little," she would say, "Rwandans all lived in big grass huts, and people told their children, 'Whatever you do, don't go into the back of the hut, where it's always dark, where we put the big jugs we always keep our backs turned to, because you might run into the *ingegera*.'" And then Mama described the *ingegera*: a little creature, very black and very thin, whose eyes glowed like red coals. He's always stark naked, or else he wears dried banana leaf tatters, and if you hear the sound of rustling leaves from behind the jugs, that means he's there. But, Mama would tell us, the most amazing thing about the *ingegera* is his hair, a tangled mop that can't be combed out (because he has no one to comb it for him or to shave his head), stiff with dirt and ash, like a clump of grass fronds and roots on the top of his head. After the evening meal, people often leave a few beans and sweet potatoes in the bottom of the kettle. But if you get up in the morning and find the kettle empty, that's because the *ingegera* is there behind the big jugs, and if you move the jugs you might well plunge your hand into a mane of filthy, matted hair and see his disheveled silhouette against the ceiling of the hut, and his long, hooked fingernails. My mother didn't know if every hut had its own *ingegera*, or if there was only one *ingegera* that went from one house to another.

Sitting beside the three stones of the hearth, my mother spun out her tales – her stories of wicked stepmothers, talking animals, the songs of the kindly old aunt – and I was the only one listening and drowsing, rocked by the interminable motherly singsong, and in my half-sleep, lulled by the heat of the fire, I said to Mama: "More! More!"

The 1960s: Hutu terror, between the militias and the soldiers

Those peaceful days were a rare thing in Nyamata. The soldiers of Gako camp were always there to remind us what we were: snakes, Inyenzi, cockroaches. Nothing human about us. One day, we'd have to be got rid of. In the meantime, the terror was systematic and organized. On the pretext of training or security checks, the soldiers endlessly patrolled the road, between the houses, in the banana groves. The soldiers pointed their weapons from the trucks that drove back and forth over the dirt roads. Sometimes they fired.

From Gitagata to the school in Nyamata, the dirt road joined up with the highway that went on to the Burundi border. All the children were in a hurry to reach school before the drum sounded. But they had an even more pressing concern: they had to listen for engines. If they heard the tiniest sound, they had just time enough to dive under the coffee plants, leap into the bush, or take cover in the first house they could find. The road to Nyamata was also the road to Gako camp. Military trucks often went by, and the soldiers fired or threw grenades to terrorize any child foolish enough to walk by the side of the road. Nothing the soldiers did on the Nyamata road was a scandal, since no one ever walked it but Tutsis.

One day there were four of us on the way to school: Jacqueline, Kayisharaza, Candida, and me. A truck suddenly appeared behind us. We hadn't heard it coming. All we could do was dive into the coffee plants. Too late! The soldiers had seen us, and they'd thrown a grenade. Kayisharaza's leg was shredded. She had to give up on school. She couldn't drag her dead leg all the way to Nyamata. She was the oldest girl in her family, and she became a burden for them, for her brothers and sisters. I don't know how many schoolchildren were wounded like that on the road to Nyamata.

And so paths had to be cleared through the brush, making the walk much longer. But the risk of running into an elephant or a buffalo frightened us far less than the thought of coming across an army truck.

A house was no sanctuary either. The soldiers often burst in, especially just before dawn or after nightfall. The sheet metal door fell to the ground with a clatter, and three or four soldiers raced inside. They brutally shoved us out; anyone unlucky enough to be slow about it was struck with a rifle butt. They lined us up along the dirt road, and while one of them kept us at bay with his rifle, the others inside scattered the straw of the beds, overturned the jugs, took the clean mats – our spare bedding – down from the walls to throw them into the mud or the dirt. They claimed to be looking for correspondence with the Inyenzi in Burundi, or photographs of Kigeri. Once they'd made sure Kayibanda's portrait was hanging in the place of honor, they went off into the night or early morning to bring terror to other houses.

Sometimes, on the contrary, they confined us inside our houses. No one knew why this curfew had been imposed, or how long it would last. Then they forbade us to farm. The children couldn't go to school. The soldiers methodically patrolled the village. Anyone careless enough to set foot outside was beaten. Life became hard if the curfew went on: there was no way to fetch water or wood. We couldn't dig sweet potatoes or cut bananas. Even the latrines, which were generally far from the houses, off in the banana grove, were off limits. Closed up in our houses, we were paralyzed with fright. We didn't dare speak.

The only seemingly inviolable refuge was the church of the Nyamata mission. As soon as we sensed some threat coming, we knew we had to get to that one place of safety. There was something reassuring in what happened next, since we'd seen it many times before. It would happen on a Sunday: the Tutsis gathered for Mass would hear the roar of a hostile crowd coming from outside the church's front door. The mob had clearly been mustered up by the local authorities, who took great care to keep their hatred at a fever pitch and incite them to violence. Sometimes the howling crowd would try to get in. Then the priest saying Mass, a German named Father Canoni – that's what we called him, at least – stepped away from the altar, took off his chasuble, went into the sacristy for his rifle, and slowly advanced toward the assailants. They hesitated for a moment, then backed away and ran off as fast as they could.

In 1994 the Tutsis of Nyamata once again sought shelter in the church, but this time there was no Father Canoni to chase off the murderers: the UN soldiers had come to evacuate the white people, and the missionaries went with them, knowing they were leaving for dead more than five thousand men, women, and children who thought they'd found sanctuary in their church.

Today the Nyamata church has become a genocide memorial. The survivors had to fight hard to keep it from becoming a place of worship again, as the Catholic higher-ups insisted. In a crypt, the skulls are lined up in neat rows, the bones carefully stacked. The sheet metal roof is peppered with bright, shiny spots where it was struck by bullets or grenade shrapnel. Against the brick wall, to the left of the altar, the Virgin of Lourdes watches over the now-empty pews, her veil red with blood. That Virgin of Nyamata was lucky. She too escaped the carnage. In many other churches, the killers shattered the statues of the Virgin. They thought she'd been given a Tutsi face. They couldn't stand the sight of her straight little nose.

—— —— ——

Things turned still worse in 1967. From the earliest days of that year, we could feel the tension rising, something dangerous coming. Among the Bagesera, the town councilors held mysterious meetings to which only Hutus were summoned. The rumor was that machetes were being handed out. Some were even distributed at the town hall, people said. Then sometime in April, maybe Easter Monday, all the adults over sixteen were called to the town hall.

I stayed home alone with my little sisters, Julienne and Jeanne. It was raining. One of those violent downpours typical of the long rainy season, transforming the dirt roads into muddy torrents. I was inside, watching over the few beans heating up in the kettle. My two little sisters were outside in spite of the rain: the corn field had to be guarded, or the monkeys would beat us to the brand-new ears. The only sound I could hear was the patter of the rain on the banana trees' huge leaves. Those banana trees grow faster because of the household waste we throw at their feet. But suddenly I made out another noise I knew well – *shuwafu! shuwafu!* – the sound of boots in the mud. I rushed outside and ran straight into two soldiers driving my two sisters along with blows from their rifle butts. The little girls collapsed at my feet. The soldiers walked into the house, ransacked it in the usual way, then disappeared.

Trembling in terror, the three of us held each other tight. I'd put the sheet metal back over the doorway, as if that might protect us.

And then came the sound of shouts and tramping feet from the road. Through the holes in the sheet metal, we saw something that left us petrified with fear: a huge crowd of soldiers heading toward Lake Cyohoha, dragging bodies that looked like broken marionettes, among which I recognized some neighbors of ours, Rwabukumba and his brother. They were young men, not yet twenty. The bodies being dragged along – not all of them corpses, some were still moving and groaning – belonged to young men, snakes, cockroaches, Inyenzi, who had to be eliminated before they could turn dangerous.

We spent the night waiting for our parents. They came back very early the next day. They never said a word. My mother always took such care to elegantly tie on her *pagne*, but now she had it draped over her head, like the Holy Virgin. She said nothing. Neither did the neighbors, when they reappeared. They took care not to cross each other's paths, they pretended they hadn't seen each other. My mother murmured a strange word, a word she didn't understand: the English word *meeting*. We weren't supposed to have meetings. And when three people greeted each other, someone murmured "meeting" and they all fled in different directions.

When we went back to school, there were bodies by the highway to Nyamata, in the ditches. Some had been thrown there, others had been swept along by the rushing rainwater. Among them we recognized Ngangure, the father of Protais, who was in my class at school. Their families had been forbidden to pick up the bodies.

No one wanted to fetch water. We didn't dare. We made do as best we could with our stored-up rainwater, but soon it ran out, and we had no choice but to head to the lake. Drawing water is traditionally the children's job, so I went off with Candida.

On the lakeshore, things had changed. There were people we hadn't seen before: very young men, adolescents, just kids in uniform. But not military uniforms: they were dressed in shorts and khaki shirts, a little like boy scouts. They didn't have rifles; they had big sticks or clubs, studded with sharp spikes. They were living in the buildings that had recently been put up by the lakeside. Until that day, we had no idea who they were meant for.

Many of those boys were posted along the shoreline, as if standing guard. When we walked into the water to fill our calabashes, we saw what they were guarding: the tied-up bodies of victims slowly dying in the shallows of the lake, little waves washing over them now and then. The newcomers were there to keep away the families who wanted to rescue their children or at least take home their bodies. For a long time we found little pieces of skin and rotting body parts in our calabashes when we fetched water.

Soon our new persecutors made themselves known: they were the revolutionary youth brigade of the single party, the MDR-Parmehutu. In truth, they were hoodlums picked up in the streets of Kigali and trained for violence and murder. They were quick learners, and soon mastered the only lesson they were ever taught: how to humiliate and terrorize a defenseless population.

Every day toward mid-morning, the youth of the single party paraded in double time, their cudgels or clubs on their shoulders. They sang at the top of their lungs, and their songs seemed to be meant for our ears. They sang the praises of Kayibanda, the emancipator of the Hutus; they celebrated the people who would forever be the majority, the only real Rwandans, authentic and indigenous, the Hutus. The parade route was always the same: from their camp on Lake Cyohoha up to Rwabashi's hut, where the dirt road met the highway from Nyamata to the Burundi border. The first half of the parade was fairly orderly, but not the return trip. Once they reached the highway and turned around, the young people of the party broke ranks and spread out along the path back to camp, turning into a violent, pillaging mob. Woe unto any careless passerby who hadn't had time to take shelter: he would be punched, thrown to the ground, beaten. The women who sold peanuts and sometimes bananas in front of their houses hurried to bundle up their wares before they could be trampled and looted. Sometimes the thugs invaded the houses, simply for the pleasure of wreaking havoc. And we heard their laughter, mingled with insults, as they boasted of their exploits.

From then on, going for water from Lake Cyohoha meant exposing yourself to all sorts of torments, because you had to pass by their camp. Coming back from the lake with our calabashes on our heads, we found our persecutors waiting. Now we were at the mercy of their sadistic whims. And they had plenty of imagination. For a little fun, they emptied our calabashes so we'd have to go back for water, then broke them when we came by again. They laughed and laughed. Or else they would line us up along the path, spit in our faces, and stomp on our feet with their big army shoes. And they laughed at the tears of the little snakes, the cockroaches, the Inyenzi. Sometimes it was more serious, their eyes were red, they weren't laughing, they beat up the boys and dragged a girl into the undergrowth behind their camp to be raped. That was why we took to fetching water only in the fierce heat of the early afternoon, while they were taking their siesta, doing our very best not to make a sound.

Of course, it was the girls that interested the young revolutionaries the most. On the way home from their parade, they would come after any girl who hadn't had time to hide. Rapes were not rare. A few poor girls became their playthings, just as young Tutsi women and girls would be during the genocide. At least there was no AIDS in those days.

The hunt for girls was especially intense after dark. At that time, I was spending the nights with my cousin Mukantwari, who might have been twenty years old. It's a custom in Rwanda for girls to share the bed of young women of marriageable age. This is especially common among cousins: they spend the night telling stories, posing riddles, making fun of boys, and laughing without end.

My cousin lived with her grandmother Bureriya, a bent-over old woman she kept company. Her parents lived across the way. Her father Ngoboka was a very strong man, afraid of no one. He had an axe that kept away anyone who might mean him harm.

More than once, the Parmehutu youth tried to get their hands on Mukantwari. As soon as we heard them coming, Mukantwari and I would dive under her grandmother's bed while the old lady brandished her little stick and shouted, as loud as she could: "Go away! Go away!" She snatched up a burning branch from the hearth and waved it in the assailants' faces.

Hearing her shouts, Ngoboka – whose name means nothing other than "He-who-comes-when-he-is-needed-most" – came running and drove off the would-be abductors, whose bravery did not extend to confronting a colossus and his terrible axe appearing all at once in the night.

The Tutsi girls fascinated the Hutus. Their leaders set the example: marrying a Tutsi was one of the privileges of the victors. They came to Nyamata to take their pick.

In Nyamata, then called the municipality of Kanzenze, the mayor was the first one to do so. He was a Hutu, "from Rwanda," as we said. No one educated enough for that post had been found among the Bagesera. The mayor was an old bachelor. No one knew why he'd never married. But in Nyamata it wasn't hard to find a wife. He set his sights on Banayija, a very beautiful girl whose impoverished mother supported herself and her four daughters by selling loose cigarettes and sorghum or banana beer. When the mayor came for her daughter, he didn't ask Banayija's opinion, or her mother's. "The Tutsis and their daughters have lost the right to be proud," he liked to say. And he went off with Banayija.

Many others came to help themselves in Nyamata. Any girl whose beauty put her in danger was hidden away. Often, though, the parents felt so threatened that they didn't dare refuse. Besides, handing a daughter over to the persecutors might mean saving the family.

1968: The national exam, unhoped-for success

After six years of primary school, students found themselves facing a formidable barrier: the famous and dreaded national examination, the competitive test you had to pass at all costs if you wanted to be among the select few admitted to secondary school. The challenge was even more daunting for Tutsis, because the ethnic quotas put in place by the Hutu regime allowed them no more than ten percent of the admissions. That percentage had been grudgingly granted, and was often applied according to criteria that had nothing to do with the scores. We in Nyamata never came close to the fateful quota: most years, not a single candidate from Nyamata was named on the lists.

It was in 1968 that I took the national exam. Obviously, no one had any illusions about the results, but that didn't stop the students from studying hard, nor the teachers from encouraging them, nor the parents from hoping. Nonetheless, we knew perfectly well that of the five hundred-some students taking the test in Nyamata, we would be able to count those who passed on the fingers of one hand.

When the morning of the exam came, I was firmly resolved not to take it. I claimed I'd come down with *agapfura* – a sore throat. I suddenly developed an irresistible zeal for housework; it was vitally urgent that I sweep the yard and fetch water – far more urgent than walking ten kilometers to take a test I had no chance of passing. My mother was about to give in, but my father didn't see things that way. His children's scholarly success meant more to him than anything. He thought that might give his family some chance of surviving, of being spared. He clung to that illusion for all he was worth. André and Alexia had gone on to secondary school before the ethnic apartheid was imposed. Now it was my turn. Like them, I would keep up my studies.

In a tone that allowed no objection, my father ordered me, "Get ready, and be quick about it." I splashed water on my face, washed my feet – there wasn't enough water that morning for anything more. I put on my school dress. My father had already tied on his white *pagne*, shouldered his stick, and now he was pushing me out onto the road to Nyamata.

As usual, they'd set up a testing room in the mission. The three classes of the Nyamata primary school were there, along with the classes from Cyugaro, Ntarama, and Musenyi. You had to be good at French, at math, you had to know the names of the ministers, the date of Rwanda's independence, the role of the Party . . . You had to be smart, but not too smart. Everyone had noticed long before that the best students never passed. Better to stick to an unremarkable average grade. In any case, the standards they used to pick the winners from Nyamata remained deeply mysterious to us.

We waited to hear the results all through the long vacation. They would be announced on the radio, when the new school year was near. We didn't have a radio in our house, but that was of little concern to me. At twelve years old, I'd come to accept the idea that I would always be a peasant. In my torn *pagne*, a filthy scarf tied around my head, I would hoe the earth. I would do that all my life, assuming they let me live.

―― ―― ――

One afternoon, just after the meal, we were outside in the shade of the big manioc tree, resting and shelling beans. All at once a crowd appeared at the end of the dirt road. They seemed to be celebrating. There were women, girls, children dancing. And they were shouting, and as they came toward us, we made out what they were shouting: "Mukasonga! Mukasonga!" They poured into our yard. Leading the parade was the Gitagata merchant who sold cigarettes, gasoline, and boxes of matches from his tiny shop. He was the only one in the village with a radio, and he explained, breathless with emotion, that he'd heard my name announced, Mukasonga Skolastika, and not only had she passed the exam, but she was enrolled in the Lycée Notre Dame de Cîteaux, the secondary school in the capital, the best in all Rwanda. *"Yatsinze! Yatsinze!"* the crowd cried, "Mukasonga passed!"

I couldn't understand what was happening. My mother knocked over her basket of beans and began to cry. Then I burst into tears myself. For some reason, my brother André was spitting insults at me. My father, who was taking his siesta, came out of the house wrapped in his covers. He raised his stick as if to strike me. All my sisters were crying. And the crowd was shouting and dancing.

A spontaneous party came together in our yard. The neighbors brought what they could: peanuts, corn. The old women hugged me. The girls and children danced. I danced with them. It wasn't just my success they were celebrating, it was the whole village's! A little later, my godmother Angelina came to confirm the good news. She lived far away, in Gitwe. Her husband was a teacher, and he had a radio. As soon as she heard my name, she set off running, and all along the road, she was shouting, "Mukasonga! Mukasonga! *Yatsinze!*"

We had a great deal of trouble coming up with the six hundred francs of the *minerval*, the tuition fees, and putting together the supplies required of boarders at the school: a blanket, a pair of sheets, a bath towel, a piece of soap, a little bucket. The village tailor sewed me a nightshirt and two pairs of panties, as long as boxer shorts – the first I ever had. My father sold our bunches of ripe bananas and set aside what little money we'd earned from the coffee harvest. But even with all that, he could still only buy me one sheet: it was the start of my third year before we managed to buy the other. Everyone in Gitagata contributed, making up more than half the cost of the supplies. I was no longer the daughter of Cosma and Stefania; I was the daughter of the whole little community of Gitagata and Gitwe.

Finally the great day came, the first day of school. We had to set off early in the morning if we wanted to reach Kigali before nightfall. Even for a good walker like me, forty-five kilometers was a serious hike. My father came with me. But first we had to say goodbye to the neighbors. This took a long time: so many greetings, so much advice to be given. Finally the women untied the knots on their *pagnes*, which they used as purses, and gave me a few coins or a crumpled little bill. And then we were off, we crossed the big bridge over the Nyabarongo. I was on my way to another world.

1968-1971:
A humiliated student

Arriving at the Lycée Notre-Dame-de-Cîteaux with the little card-board suitcase once used by my brother André, and then by Alexia, I was filled with hope and apprehension at the same time. My apprehensions were more than justified, but I never lost hope.

I'd seen violent and even deadly persecution in Nyamata, but the solidarity of the ghetto gave us the strength to endure it. At school, I would know the solitude of humiliation and rejection.

I hadn't shed my Tutsi status when I crossed the Nyabarongo – anything but. And in any case, there was no way to hide it. Every student was issued an ID card marked with their so-called ethnic group, like a brand on a cow. When I was forced to show it to one of the sisters, her look and her attitude changed immediately: wariness, disdain, or hatred? I didn't want to know. They also discovered that I came from Nyamata. I wasn't only a Tutsi: I was an Inyenzi, one of those cockroaches they'd expelled from the livable part of Rwanda, and perhaps from the human race. Among my schoolmates, too, I soon came to feel different. Or rather, it was they who made that difference cruelly clear to me. They made me ashamed of the color of my skin (not dark enough for their tastes), of my nose (too straight, they said), and of my hair (too much of it). It was my hair that caused me the most trouble. Evidently it was Ethiopian hair, *irende*, the supposed mark of the Inyenzi. I spent my time putting water on that Inyenzi hair so it would shrink down to a little ball, tight as a sponge. Most often, I resigned myself to shaving it off. That hurt me: in spite of the mockery, I was fond of my hair.

They divided us up into teams, and we took turns doing the dishes, cleaning the refectory or the dormitories. The team leader was always a third-year girl. My leader was named Pascasie. I was the only Tutsi on the team. Pascasie and the rest took an immediate dislike to me. The hardest chores always fell to me. In fact, I soon realized it wasn't my place to wait for orders. I always volunteered. As the mayor of Nyamata had said, the Tutsis had lost the right to be proud.

The teams all ate at the same table. Mealtimes were the hardest part of the day for me. A thousand times, I wished I didn't have to eat. My throat went tight with terror whenever a meal was near. We walked into the refectory in silence. We prayed, and then sat down in silence. A bell signaled that it was time to begin eating, and we had permission to talk. The room filled with the sound of conversation, but no one ever spoke to me. I could feel them staring at me, telling me I wasn't supposed to be there, that my presence disgusted them, that it wasn't by choice that they were living – and, even worse, eating – with an Inyenzi, a cockroach. I grew used to serving myself after all the others. When there were bananas or sweet potatoes, there was nothing left in the dish by the time it came to me, and I had to make do with the maggot-ridden beans no one would touch. And I grew used to peeling the sweet potatoes in the others' place, doing the dishes, cleaning the toilets. I never rebelled, even if I wept when no one was looking. I found all this almost normal. A strange curse hung over me. I was a Tutsi. Worse yet, I was from Nyamata, I was an Inyenzi. I wasn't supposed to be there at the Lycée Notre-Dame-de-Cîteaux. It was a mistake, an oversight on the part of those who'd expelled us from the Rwandan community, the people of the majority. For that reason, I made myself a paragon of zeal. I was always on the front bench at Mass, I was first in line for confession. I wanted to be beyond reproach. I was convinced that good grades alone could protect me.

Sometimes I think I never slept in all those three years at the school. At home the nights were short, but at school there was no such thing as night. The few other Tutsi students knew as well as I did that they had to be among the best, and so they worked night and day, particularly night. When dinner was done, a bell rang. We headed off to the dormitories. We washed our feet as we entered, then took our places by the bunk beds. A bell rang. We knelt. We prayed. A bell rang. We turned back our bedspreads. We got into bed. I slipped very carefully under the covers, letting no one see that I had only one sheet. The monitor made a few more rounds to silence the chatter, and then the lights were turned out.

But we Tutsis were waiting for our moment. We waited until everyone was sound asleep, until no one was getting up to go to the bathroom, until the sisters had gone off for the night. Then Agnès, who was in her third year, shook the piece of green canvas that was our standard-issue bedspread: this was the signal. We quietly got out of bed, wrapped ourselves in our bedspreads to ward off the nighttime cold, and followed after Agnès. She was a tiny girl, and her bedspread dragged behind her on the ground: we called her Monseigneur. The silent parade ended in the bathroom, the only place where a nightlight stayed on all through the night. We gently closed the door, and one of us sat down with her back pressed against it, in case someone came along. We had our study room for the night. Often we studied our lessons and did our homework until morning. Everything I learned at Notre-Dame-de-Cîteaux I learned in the toilet.

The teachers seemed to be completely faithful to the regime and the system. Most of them were Belgian, except the French teacher, who was French, and the English teacher, who was English. The only Rwandan was the Kinyarwanda teacher, Victoria, a Tutsi. In any case, we had to beware of the teachers. The older girls had warned us of that as soon as we got there by telling us the story of Sylvia. Sylvia was from Nyamata. In a composition – I never found out what the subject was – she made the mistake of alluding to the displaced people of Nyamata and calling for fairer treatment. They said the paper was immediately sent on to the Mother Superior, Sister Béatrice. And Sylvia was expelled. You were supposed to say that Rwanda was a country blessed by God, as the priests claimed. That Kayibanda had created a little paradise in the heart of Africa. A waiting room for heaven. Before he came along, there was only darkness and barbarity. I memorized the islands and the cities of Japan: Hokkaido, Nagasaki, Yokohama . . . It sounded like Kinyarwanda.

—— —— ——

The first year was the worst, but in time my quarantine turned a little less harsh. A third-year girl, Immaculée Nyirabyago, who later married a minister in the Habyarimana government, took me under her wing. She was from Kigali, a real city girl! They said her father was a Tutsi (her mother was Hutu), but she was, if I can put it like this, a "fashionable girl." Everyone was drawn to her, her schoolmates and teachers alike. A little clique had formed around her, made up of all the daughters of ministers, company directors, important people. There was also Assumpta, President Kayibanda's daughter.

It must be said that I spared no effort to gain Immaculée's protection, if not her friendship. I offered her my services: risking expulsion, I used to sneak out of the school to go and buy sugar for her at the market.

At breakfast, the very watery milk furnished by the WFP was not sugared. If you wanted sugar, you had to get it for yourself, so anyone who had money used the free time between a meal and the next class to slip out to the market and buy some. Immaculée promised she'd give me a little if I went in her place. Off I went, then, not so much to buy sugar as to safeguard her "friendship."

At that time, which must have been 1971, there was major roadwork being done between the school and the market. There were huge piles of dirt everywhere. All you had to do was climb up a pile and slide down the other side, and you were in the middle of the market. Just like a playground slide! I brought back the sugar, terrified that sister Kisito, the pitiless monitor, might catch me, but also proud of my exploit, which strengthened my bonds with my protectress.

Having found a place under Immaculée's wing, I was sometimes allowed into the little clique of privileged girls. I wasn't really a part of it, of course, and I never felt at ease in their midst. We all wore the same uniform, but still there was no bridging the distance between us. They left the school whenever they pleased, they were never in a hurry to get back to the classroom, they never hesitated to challenge the teachers. No one ever rebuked them. But above all, they had shoes – some of them with high heels! I myself went barefoot. It wasn't until the end of my third year, by cheating on the *minerval*, that I was able to buy a pair of *kambambili*, what I believe are called flip-flops in English, my first shoes!

Immaculée's friends' attitude toward me was deeply ambiguous. Many of them had Tutsi mothers, women forced to marry men in power. The girls were Hutu, of course, since their fathers were. But it seemed as if they felt a need to shake off the hereditary stain of having a Tutsi for a mother. And so they often tried to top each other in their scorn and cruelty toward their Tutsi schoolmates. Sometimes, on the other hand, they seemed to want to befriend them, and to forge mysteriously cordial bonds. That was how I went one day to eat manioc paste at the Kayibanda house.

On Sunday afternoons, we were allowed to leave the school. I generally didn't take advantage of that freedom, and stayed behind to work. But sometimes, at Immaculée's urging, I went with the little clique to one of the girls' houses for a meal of manioc paste. Manioc paste was considered the "civilized" dish *par excellence*, something reserved for city-dwellers, a little like champagne in France. Like all the others, Assumpta sometimes invited her friends to her house – the President's house! I still wonder why Immaculée and her friends brought me along. Did they think it would be funny? Was it a dare? Were they trying to humiliate me? I had a knot in my stomach when we came to the military checkpoints around the presidential residence. There was no way to distinguish me from the others by my size or my face, but I couldn't stop thinking about my hair. I was sure it would give me away, that the soldiers would seize me because of my hair. Nevertheless, I walked straight through the checkpoint with the other girls, to whom the soldiers gave a friendly greeting, and found myself in the kitchen of the President of the Republic. "Stay right here," my schoolmates said, "and whatever you do, don't go into the living room. The President mustn't see you." I ate my manioc paste in the kitchen. If the President's wife Viridiana happened to come in, there was nothing to worry about: she was a Tutsi.

———   ———   ———

And then there were the vacations, the joy of going back home to my family, the party Gitagata would throw for the return of its "intellectuals." I would dance with the girls who'd stayed in the village—how I loved to dance! Laughing, they would tell me all the village gossip, and I would tell them the news from the city. I would pick up the mattock again, alongside my mother. I wouldn't miss the sorghum harvest. But before all that, there was a terrible ordeal to endure: crossing the big bridge over the Nyabarongo.

And so, on the first day of vacation, the three or four girls from Nyamata all set off together. We ran, we had to be there before dark. Sometimes we weren't let out of school until after lunch, so instead of the main road home, through Kicukiro, we took a short cut that went straight to Gahanga. But for that we had to walk past the camp.

We didn't know what might happen if the soldiers asked for our ID cards. We took a thousand precautions to get by without being seen. Then we plunged into the valley, we climbed up Mburabuturo hill, we ran, we ran, we barreled down the slopes of the Gahanga sector toward the valley of the Nyabarongo, and we saw the big iron bridge, the reddish water, the papyrus plants in the swamps. We also saw the barricade at the bridge's entrance, and the soldiers slumped in their chairs, the rifles between their legs, the beer bottles scattered at their feet.

They'd seen us coming. They knew who we were: we were Inyenzi from Nyamata. There was no point trying to hide our hair, trying to make ourselves inconspicuous: they were waiting for us. We scarcely dared to go on, but we had to cross the bridge. The soldiers were already snickering as they saw us timidly inching toward them. They shouted at us, "Inyenzis, lower your heads, don't show your faces, don't show your noses, we don't want to see that, whatever you do don't look us in the eye, come forward but keep your heads down, never forget, you're Inyenzi." We held out our papers, and the humiliations began. Depending on their mood or their fancies, they might spit in our faces, or kick us with their heavy boots, or strike us with their rifle butts. They dragged us to the bank of the Nyabarongo and forced us to look down into the muddy water, as red as if it had been tainted with blood: "Look closely," they cried, "that's where you're going to end up, all you cockroaches, you Inyenzi, one day you'll all be thrown into that water."

1971-1973: The School of Social Work in Butare, the illusion of a normal life

At the end of the first two years, there was a competitive exam for admission to the humanities program, which is to say the second half of university study, or to the professional schools. Every candidate had to state three choices, in order of preference: one of them would be granted, depending on the test results and the ranking. As my first choice, I put down the School of Social Work in Butare, with a note that I meant not the two-year auxiliary course, but the four-year course for full-fledged social workers. All my friends laughed at me, telling me I'd never be admitted, even with my good grades: the Butare School of Social Work was not for the Inyenzi of Nyamata.

Nevertheless, I was admitted to the full four-year program, starting in the fall of 1971. There were some thirty of us in my entering class. There were six Tutsis: Aimable, Perpétue, Thérèse, Brigitte, Anasthasie, and me. But very soon I found that, unlike at school in Kigali, "ethnic" differences were of no concern at Butare, not to the nuns who ran the school, and not to the teachers, most of whom were Canadian. The atmosphere was relaxed, and the freedoms and comfort the students enjoyed were a revelation for me. So, in the midst of the pious, racist ghetto that was Rwanda, one little island had been spared, a place where you could find a normal life by your work alone! Needless to say, some of my Hutu classmates didn't appreciate having Tutsis in the school. Some of them watched us like hawks. Everything we did or said was reported to a third-year student, a certain Immaculée, nicknamed the Mastodon because of her imposing size, who had appointed herself political komissar and liked to boast of her closeness to the *député* Mukakayange Angela, an alumna of our school. But their spying didn't worry me. Inside the school I felt safe, as if my grades had erased the word "Tutsi" from my ID card. I was convinced that this school was my long awaited lucky break, that the curse hanging over me had finally been lifted.

It must be said that the School of Social Work strove to play a pioneering role in the promotion of women. The few women who had become *députés* or ministers (there were always one or two female

89

ministers in the government) had studied there. Now and then one of those great ladies would pay us a visit, and no doubt some of us were already picturing ourselves in the presidential box on Independence Day.

But our curriculum didn't set out to prepare us for politics or social life. The goal was to make us a real force for Rwanda's development, able to adapt to any milieu, especially the countryside, so there were many practical courses in addition to French, math, and English. There was carpentry: starting from a block of wood, we had to put together a bench, making more or less skillful use of a saw and a hammer. In animal sciences, we didn't limit ourselves to theory: we had to build a rabbit hutch, and we had to go and feed the pigs in their sties. We had hands-on training in agriculture: every student was responsible for the plot assigned to her in the school's huge gardens. We took a personal interest in the success of our plantings, since those were the vegetables we ate at meals. We were better equipped than the peasants in the hills, it's true. We had a mattock, of course, but also a hoe, a Dutch hoe, a harrow . . . And then there was the wheelbarrow, an infernal device that insisted on zigzagging every which way with its load of manure, no matter how I struggled. Nor was hygiene forgotten: there was a Belgian teacher who specialized in latrines. Under his direction, we dug the trench, laid the foundation. But the latrines were never finished. That teacher spent too long on theory. Needless to say, we called him Monsieur Musarane – Monsieur Latrines.

Mademoiselle Barbe, a Frenchwoman, introduced us to civilized cuisine, which was based on mayonnaise. I became an expert in beating it with a fork in the bowl. I still haven't lost my touch. Mademoiselle Barbe undertook to initiate us into the mysteries of sauerkraut. We scrupulously followed her instructions, taking care not to seem too surprised: cut up the cabbage, put it in a bucket, set a rock on the top to keep it tamped down. But I rebelled when we had to empty a bottle of beer into the bucket, a bottle of Primus, that precious potion we could never afford, not even with the earnings from the coffee harvest, a drink given only to the gravely ill in the direst of circumstances. I had to hold back my tears as I poured out the beer: how I wished I could filch it to give to my father! But that was impossible. Mademoiselle Barbe followed her recipe to the letter. Then we had to watch over the fermentation, taste the cabbage. Mademoiselle Barbe swallowed it; we spat it out. Finally the great day came. The sauerkraut was ready. None of the girls would touch it. Leading by example, Mademoiselle Barbe served herself a plateful and enthusiastically ate it down. She then disappeared for a week. Some of us wanted to go and pay her a visit in her little room. Out of the question, they told us: she wasn't well. We didn't dare burst out laughing.

I've always thought that Butare was the best part of my education – the part that made me able to adapt wherever I later went, as much among the Hutu peasantwomen of Burundi as in France, in my trade as a social worker.

——— ——— ———

An unfamiliar atmosphere of freedom reigned in the school, thanks largely to one single nun, Sister Capito. She was old, but overflowing with energy and ideas. Her innovations caused a scandal in a Rwanda where the regime and the Church imposed the most narrow-minded conservatism. For instance, we had loudspeakers in the refectory and the dormitories, but they broadcast neither hymns to the Virgin nor anthems to the glory of Kayibanda; all day long, we heard songs by Claude François, Adamo, Nana Mouskouri. We were awakened by *If I Had a Hammer*. The beds in the dormitory were separated by screens, and for the first time in my life, like most of my schoolmates, I discovered the advantages of a certain amount of privacy.

Every morning a delegation of students went to draw up the day's menu, with the aid of the head cook. There was no maggoty porridge like we had at Kigali; there were bananas, vegetables, and fruit from our garden. At breakfast we had lard, standing in as butter: we eagerly waited for morning so we could wolf down pieces of bread dripping with oily fat.

For national holidays and our days out, we wore a special uniform that brought us a good deal of attention in the parades. It was tight at the waist, with chevrons underscoring the bold décolleté. There was no mistaking it, we girls from the School of Social Work were the feminine elite of our nation!

Thanks to one of Sister Capito's most daring initiatives, Butare's high-minded set – or were they simply jealous? – took to calling us *ihene*, goats, the goat being the animal emblem of wanton licentiousness. On Sunday afternoons, from two to four, the boys from the nearby secondary school were allowed to come calling on us. Oh! those visits were well chaperoned, of course. They took place in the garden: benches were put out under the bougainvillea trees, and two girls sat on each bench. Those two girls were allowed to receive only one boy. They sat waiting under the bougainvillea. The boys stood at the gate, not daring to come any further. There they stayed behind the gate, looking at us as we sat under the bougainvillea. The fourth-year girls showed a little more initiative: they went to bring the boys in themselves. But we first-year girls never moved. We never managed to get a boy to come see us. We just sat there under the bougainvillea.

My Tutsi schoolmates and I had another destination for our days off. We went to visit Queen Gicanda, the widow of King Mutara Rudahigwa, who died mysteriously in Bujumbura in 1959. We had to make very sure we weren't being followed. We took a thousand precautions. At first, we went purely out of curiosity. I had a pretext: two of her aunts were in Nyamata. I gave her news of them. Like us, Nyirakigwene and Nyiramasuka had been deported to Nyamata. They'd lost none of their regal dignity. They sat majestically face-to-face in front of their shabby sheet-metal hut, both of them crowned with diadems of white pearls and draped in immaculate *pagnes*. They received their visitors – who sat on mats laid out just like at the royal court – with noble beneficence. We scarcely said a word. It was enough just to look at them. They never went to fetch water or wood for themselves. We fought for the honor of serving them. Even the Hutus. As for Gicanda, she welcomed us like a good-hearted mother. She gave us milk to drink. It was like being transported to another world. The world we'd never known.

In 1994, the old woman was viciously attacked. I won't describe how she was humiliated, raped, tortured. I want to remember only the woman who gave us milk, Gicanda, the queen with the beautiful face.

1973: Driven from school, driven from Rwanda

At the beginning of the 1972 school year, I quickly realized things weren't the same. Our principal, Béatrice, whom we nicknamed Nyiramusambi, the "black-crowned crane," because of her long neck, had been replaced by a new principal. He was violently opposed to Sister Capito's bold ideas, and intended to impose the moral order that was the grim, hypocritical norm of a very Christian Rwanda: no more music, no more meetings with boys. One day he caught me humming a song by Nana Mouskouri, and he forced me to sing it in front of all my classmates. I nearly died of shame.

Among the new teachers there were refugees from Burundi, driven out by the bloody events of May 1972: they only heightened the mounting tension, as if there were any need. We Tutsis had developed particularly sensitive antennae to detect the early signs of a threat, and its inexorable buildup. We soon observed that the Mastodon and her political cell never came to class anymore. We saw them going back and forth in the hallways, having long whispered conversations, giving themselves important airs. They flocked around Immaculée, one of the Burundian refugees, and often they went to the beautiful yellow house she'd been lodged in, behind the post office. They had meetings well into the night in the big vacant lot separating the school from the eucalyptus woods. We knew something was coming, we knew it wouldn't be long, and we knew the Tutsi students would be in the crosshairs.

One afternoon, during math class I think, we heard a loud crash. It was the gate of the main entry being beaten down, and at almost the same moment two Tutsis in their last year opened the classroom door, shouting "Mukasonga! Mukasonga! Hurry!" Without a moment's thought, we raced into the hallway. Behind us was the same angry-mob sound I'd heard thirteen years earlier, at Magi, the same roar rushing toward me I still hear today, pursuing me in my nightmares.

We ran across the vacant lot. I don't know how, but we managed to get through the school's barbed wire fence and hide in the eucalyptus woods between the school and the Gikongoro road. From our hiding place, we saw our classmates go by, showing the boys from the secondary school the way, shouting "This time they're done for! We're going to get those Inyenzi!"

When night fell we went our separate ways to look for safer places to hide. In my case this was with Gasana, my godmother Angelina's brother, who lived in Butare. He worked and lived at the National Pedagogical Institute with his sister Margot, a university employee. I often went there to eat manioc paste. They welcomed me in and somehow got word to my sister Alexia, who was a teacher at the school of the Anglican Kigeme mission in Gikongoro. There was no question of going to Nyamata, it seemed far too dangerous. There would probably be checkpoints on the roads, and we had no idea what was going on there. Alexia came to get me. I don't remember how we reached Kigeme. But there, too, the situation was explosive. Alexia had already been threatened, and couldn't take me in. One of my sister's colleagues, I think her name was Angèle, agreed to hide me. She was a Tutsi married to a Hutu *député*. Needless to say, the master of the house wasn't told of my presence: the Tutsi wives of high-placed Hutus often protected their family members this way, by discreetly integrating them into their households. I tried to blend in with the many serving girls who worked in the back courtyard, as they did at most big Rwandan houses. One servant more or less, who would notice? When I sensed pressing danger, I slipped under a bed. Sometimes I stayed there all day. I lived like a rat.

I've always wondered how Angèle talked her husband into driving me to Kigali. Had he taken pity on me? Was the *député* afraid he might face trouble for hiding an Inyenzi under his roof, even if he didn't know it? In any case, it was in the trunk of the Hutu *député's* car that I made the trip to Kigali. They dropped me off at the bursar's office of the Mission, where I found a priest from Nyamata who took me on to the parish.

——— ——— ———

On the road to Gitagata, everyone ran toward me, in tears. There was one name on everyone's lips: "Régis! Régis!" That was the name of a neighbor, a son of Kagango, the sculptor who carved beautiful female heads on canes. Régis and I had been in the same classes at primary school, and then he left for the little seminary in Kabgayi. As I walked on, I learned in bits and pieces of his horrible death. There too, the Hutu students had launched a sudden attack on their Tutsi schoolmates, before the eyes of the missionaries who taught them. Régis managed to get away, but then he carelessly set out on the main road to Kigali. The Hutu seminarians caught up with him and brought him back to Kabgayi. There they shaved him with pieces of glass and stoned him to death. An unending lament accompanied me all along the road: "Régis! Régis!"

As soon as I was home, my parents forbade me to go out again. They were more silent than ever. It was as if the walls had eyes and ears. We avoided talking to even the closest neighbors, people we shared everything with. As my mother said again and again, we mustn't have "meetings." We closed up the sheet-metal door well before nightfall. We talked in low tones.

André was teaching at the Shyogwe secondary school, and somehow he got back to the house, followed by Alexia a few days later. The whole family was safe and sound. Now the parents could tell us their plan.

Alexia, André, and I were unlucky enough to be enrolled in school. We had to leave for Burundi. Rwanda had become too dangerous for us. We escaped this time, but we would be killed in the end. Maybe tomorrow.

André was particularly unwelcome in Nyamata. Unfortunately for him, when he was at middle school in Zaza he was a classmate of Fidèle Rwambuka, an Umugesera who would later be mayor of Nyamata. Together they used to walk the long road to Zaza, far away in the Gisaka province, near the border with Tanzania. Fidèle was the bigger of the two, and so took André under his wing: he helped him with his little suitcase, and sometimes he even carried him on his back. When vacation time came around again, he went out of his way to see him back home. My mother never tired of praising Fidèle: such a nice boy, so thoughtful! But now Fidèle Rwambuka was the mayor of the Kanzenze municipality, as Nyamata was officially known, and it was best that he let his childhood friendship with a Tutsi be forgotten.

There was nothing for us to do but leave. In Burundi we could probably continue our studies and find work. And above all – my parents weren't quite sure how to say it – at least some of us had to survive, to keep the memory alive, so the family would go on, somewhere else.

We'd been chosen to survive.

We spent hours trying to decide who would go. Julienne wanted to come with us. She was too little, it was too dangerous. She'd join us later. But we couldn't leave our parents alone. They'd placed all their hopes in their children's studies as a solution to the family's misfortunes, they saw success in school as a way around the ethnic curse. Our big brother Antoine had given up on school so he could stay with our parents in the first years at Nyamata. André and Alexia decided that one of them would now stay and help out our parents in turn. It was Alexia who chose to stay. André and I were going to Burundi.

———— ———— ————

We were counting on Antoine to lead us to the border. He was working at the Karama Agricultural Institute as a gardener. He only came back to the house on Saturday evenings, riding his bicycle. That Saturday, we gathered around the jug of sorghum beer my mother always saved for her eldest son's return. Antoine told us he didn't know much about the bush, he always kept to the dirt roads on his bike, but his friend Froduald, whom I've already mentioned – he worked for the campaign to eradicate the tsetse fly – would make an ideal guide across the border into Burundi. Froduald was like a brother to him, and he was sure he wouldn't refuse. And indeed, Froduald agreed at once.

The day set for our departure came all too soon. The plan was to leave in the very middle of the night, once we were sure all the neighbors were sound asleep – not because we were afraid of being reported, but because if the neighbors saw us leaving, they might want to come with us. There was no way to leave in a large group, we'd soon be spotted by the patrolling soldiers from Gako, and we had every reason to fear that those who stayed behind would face reprisals.

With his first paycheck, my brother had bought a little cassette player. It was his pride and joy. All the neighbors came running when he played cassettes, everyone sang and danced. I remember one song that came back again and again. I can still recall a few lines of the chorus: "For the end of the world, take your suitcase, in your suitcase take just a shirt . . . " That song was for us: for us too, it was the end of the world in a way, only we were leaving without suitcases.

As soon as the neighbors were all in their houses, we closed the door and pretended to sleep. Froduald came along. My father said the rosary, walking around the banana grove behind the house, counting off the Hail Marys. My mother usually refused to join in these processions, but just this once she followed him. I think I did too.

The time came to leave. We had to be over the border before dawn; Froduald said we'd need to walk quickly. We certainly wouldn't be weighed down by luggage. In addition to his little canvas bag with his shirt and his pair of shorts, André kept his two treasures pressed close to his chest: his diploma, carefully rolled into a plastic tube, and his cassette player. I myself had only the clothes on my back. I'd abandoned my cardboard suitcase while I was fleeing Butare. All I could save were the old high-heeled shoes Immaculée had given me at school. They meant so much to me that I'd foolishly run away in them, to be sure they wouldn't be lost. My father entrusted me with his most precious possession, the jewel of the house, the bottle of Benedictine: the royal flask, somewhat fallen from its lofty rank, would be our canteen for the trip.

Antoine accompanied us to the far end of the field, and then, in the pouring rain, we set off into the night. The rain was actually a blessing: the soldiers from Gako wouldn't want to be out patrolling in such a downpour. Froduald never hesitated, the bush had no secrets for him. Around us we heard the usual clamor of the savannah: howls, birds taking flight, pounding hooves . . . A form darker than the darkness around us, a huge mass I'd taken for a hill, began to move all at once: it was a couple of elephants, majestically strolling along. "Hurry, hurry," Froduald said again and again. I limped along as quickly as I could behind my two companions. The heel of one of my shoes had broken. With great difficulty, we forced our way through the dense thickets. The thorns tore my hands, face, and feet. Day was breaking. For a moment the sun broke through the enormous clouds. As far as the eye could see, there was nothing but brambles. "This is it," said Froduald, "you're here. We're in Burundi. Keep going straight ahead and you'll end up in Kirundo." We embraced. We were all weeping. Froduald turned and went back the way he came. He wouldn't be killed that morning. He would be killed twenty years later.

1973: A refugee in Burundi

We hoped we'd soon be in Kirundo, the first town in Burundi past the border. But between the border and Kirundo lies an uninhabited wilderness, exactly like in Rwanda, not easy to find your way through. We were afraid we might be walking in circles, or retracing our steps and not knowing it. After wandering on for a long time – we were exhausted, and I was limping ever more slowly behind my brother – we joined up with a group of refugees who said they'd come from Butare, and then we finally ran into some Burundians who told us to follow them when they saw who we were. They led us to a vast camp. In a chopped-down banana grove stood a huge shelter, covered with leaves, refugees huddled beneath it. They were young, like us. They were numb with cold and soaked to the bone, because the roof of fronds offered little protection from the rain. Among them was Gasana, my godmother's brother, who'd given me shelter in Butare. He made room for us beside him, and I collapsed exhausted onto the leaves they were using as mattresses.

We stayed there for several days. The rain never stopped. We were covered with mud. There was nothing to eat but green bananas. A nauseating odor streamed from the nearby bushes. Nonetheless, we were happy. At least no one would kill us here in the mud and the stench. It was as if we'd just won a battle: we'd survived. And it was true: we didn't yet quite know it, but we were already survivors.

The Burundian authorities finally directed us to Kirundo. Functionaries and students were housed in the town's one hotel. The Auberge du Nord, run by Murara. He was Rwandan. He and his daughters did all they could to offer their poor compatriots the best possible welcome. There were some ten of us to a room. The food was good. The Murara family was very attentive to our needs. It felt almost like being on vacation. This went on for something like two weeks. Then trucks came to take us to Bujumbura. They dropped us off at a camp set up at the entrance to the Bwiza neighborhood. Now we were real refugees.

The camp seemed to be more or less run by Rukeba, the ultimate Inyenzi, a Hutu who remained faithful to the king. He strode through the camp, taking notes on the big registers he always had with him: he claimed he could tell a genuine Tutsi from an imposter. He would unmask any traitor who'd slipped into our midst. He wanted to enlist all the others, the real Tutsis, and organize them so he could lead them back home. The new exiles were unimpressed by his activist talk. Only in our studies, we thought, could we find refuge and perhaps later revenge: no matter what, it was vital that we stay in school.

The refugees were housed in big hangars, probably disused warehouses. The hygienic conditions were deplorable. Dysentery was rife, and there was even talk of cholera. And so, with five of his colleagues, André decided to rent a room in the Bwiza neighborhood. We all contributed the little money we'd managed to bring with us. My mother had given us the money she'd saved up selling bananas and peanuts. She always had a little cash hidden away in the house, for unforeseen events. She hid coins and sometimes crumpled bills in a little hole she'd made under her bed. In 1994, after they'd killed her, the murderers must have got hold of that meager nest-egg as they were destroying the house, unless she'd tried to use that pittance to buy the life of her grandchildren, Antoine's children, who lived close by.

There were twelve of us in that little rented room: six boys, six girls. André's friends had each brought one sister. In any case, the money soon ran out, and we had to give up our room. Fortunately for us, the Burundian authorities proved welcoming and generous with the Rwandan refugees. They gave jobs to any teacher who asked, and the students were enrolled in the Burundian educational system without too many formalities. Some of us took advantage of that to go back to studies we'd been forced to interrupt. André took the necessary steps and was named a teacher at the little seminary in Muyinga, in the east of the country. I enrolled in the School of Social Work in Gitega. After taking a test, I was admitted to the third year.

André and I were alone. We had no family in Burundi, and almost no one we knew. The Rwandans who'd moved there in the sixties gave us a lukewarm welcome; for them, we were showing up very late. With no one to count on, we had to look after ourselves, so we came up with a plan. My brother had decided to continue his studies. He'd always dreamt of becoming a doctor. What was impossible in Rwanda might well be feasible in Burundi. But first I had to get my degree as a social worker and find a job. As long as I was in school, André would work to support us and pay for my studies; once I finished and found a job, once I was self-sufficient, he'd go back to school. Then it would be my turn to support him.

We followed our plan to the letter. I thought only of working hard and succeeding in school, so André could go back to his studies. There were five girls from Rwanda at the school; needless to say, we were inseparable. But my Hutu schoolmates whose families had been hit by the 1972 massacres soon sought me out. We considered ourselves victims of the same "ethnic" madness. That brought us together. It was the same with the peasants I did rural outreach for. The widows welcomed me warmly, they saw me as just one more unlucky exile hounded by the implacable fate that had pursued both our peoples, in Rwanda as in Burundi, and that was now leading them into the depths of horror while we women helplessly looked on.

I earned my social work degree in June 1975. In October, my brother enrolled in medical school in Bujumbura. The school had just opened. The students did their first two years there, and then, after a very selective competition, the best students went to finish their coursework in Dakar. André was among those who earned a ticket to Senegal. He finished his medical studies there, with many specializations. For those lucky enough to have a place in school, study was the great refuge.

I was hired to a UNICEF rural development program in Gitega province, whose goal was to fight childhood malnutrition. The idea was to teach women how to grow vegetables, as well as soybeans, which are rich in proteins. I trained rural outreach leaders, who brought together all the local women who wanted to improve their own lot and their children's. I liked that work in the hills. I chose a big tree, which I pompously dubbed the "outreach center," and the women gathered around it with their babies. I unrolled my *pagne*, printed with Zairean designs. I knotted it over my jeans. Sister Mariette, the head of the school in Gitega, had taught me that I had to be as close as possible to the audience. As custom dictated, I greeted the little circle of women three times, repeating the words, *"Tugire amahoro* – let us have peace." I propped up my visual aids on the grass: big posters lent by the Health Center of Gitega, showing, for example, a stunted child gnawing on a sweet potato, while another, chubby faced and plump, smiled over a dish of beans in soy broth. Then we went on to practical applications. We gathered up the products and utensils the women had brought, to which I added my own: soybean flour, soybean oil, powdered milk. We made dishes according to the methods I'd carefully explained, illustrated by the pictures, which fascinated my audience. The teaching session soon turned into a big picnic, which took on the air of a village festival. Even some men came to join us, especially widowers. It's true that no effort was spared to whip up the curiosity of the village women: the pictures, the meal on the grass, the Land Rover and its driver. Sometimes I brought along a vaccination team from the WHO. The mothers had to be convinced to have their children vaccinated. We talked about that for a long time. Sometimes people made fun of my Rwandan way of talking, but they liked me, and they trusted me.

It was in the hills of Giheta that I met Claude, my husband, a Frenchman. With a team of Burundian researchers, he was cataloguing the traditions preserved in the memories of the elders. We went to visit the drummers together, we sought out the circles of old fig trees that, in Burundi as in Rwanda, are living vestiges of the great enclosures of the past.

The UNICEF program was only planned to last three years, and it wasn't renewed. That's how it goes with international aid programs. I then worked for a program run by the World Bank, which opened schools to educate the young people rejected by the school system. I got married. I had two sons. My brother was head doctor at the hospital of Thiès, in Senegal. My husband was appointed to Djibouti. Life seemed to be pulling me away from Rwanda. Nothing of Rwanda was left in me but a wound that could never be healed.

Rwanda: A forbidden land

For a long time I had no news of my parents, my brother, my sisters who'd stayed behind in Nyamata. Writing them was out of the question. Letters from Burundi were considered suspicious and could cause their addressees serious trouble. I kept an ear out for rumors and news from Rwanda. I urgently questioned anyone who'd dared to go there. Not until André was in Senegal could he get a letter through to our parents to tell them of our new lives. Evidently mail from West Africa wasn't thought to be dangerous.

It must have been after they got that letter that my parents allowed Julienne to come join me. After 1973, the young people of Nyamata had no access to secondary education. Those who insisted on continuing their studies were sent to what were called "complementary" schools. There the girls learned sewing, cooking, and a few rudimentary notions of French. Obviously, that didn't do much for them, and especially didn't get them a job. Julienne wanted a chance to make something of herself. In the end, my parents realized there was no other way, and so I saw Julienne arrive in Gitega. Jeanne came to join us a little later. I don't know how, but she'd got a permit to cross the border. In her case, though, she was only coming for a visit.

I'd never given up on my plan to see my parents again. As soon as I'd arrived in Bujumbura, I'd tried to get back to Rwanda. With three friends, newly exiled like me, I went to a border post by the Kanyaru River, on the main road from Bujumbura to Butare. We thought girls might be allowed back in without too much trouble. The Burundian police were willing to let us through, but they strongly advised us against it. What was going on beyond the Kanyaru was not good news for us, they said. Resigned, we started back for Bujumbura.

Julienne and I decided to accompany Jeanne back to Rwanda. Obviously, we wouldn't go by way of a border post. Once we were in Rwanda my sisters would have no problems, or at least no more than were usually caused by the word "Tutsi" on your papers. I, on the other hand, had left the country before I turned eighteen, and so I didn't have the all-important national and "ethnic" identity card that every Rwandan was obliged to carry at all times. Still, I was hoping I could go unnoticed between my sisters, and that was more or less what happened.

We'd crossed the border on a little path outside of Kirundo and before long came to a dirt road and a sizeable crowd walking to the big market in Ruhuha. Using a big mud-spattered pagne to hide anything that might give us away as city people, we fell in with the women carrying bananas or baskets of beans on their heads. In Ruhuha, we found seats in the back of one of the Toyota pickup trucks that took people to and from Nyamata. But no matter how inconspicuous and discreet we tried to be, there among the other passengers' bundles and baskets, we knew we'd have to face the soldiers from Gako, and we'd have to show them our papers.

The truck stopped at the Gako checkpoint, and all the passengers held out their ID cards to the two soldiers. Our turn comes. I pretend to be looking for my card. After a long search, growing ever more frantic, I say to Jeanne, "Jeanne, you've got my card, let me have it." Jeanne hands me her card. "No, that's not mine. I may not know how to read, but I still know my own picture." I get angry, then furious, and soon I'm on the verge of physically attacking my sister. At first amused by all this to-do, the soldiers grow bored, and in the end tell us, "OK, enough, go on." To our great relief, the Gako roadblock finally opens.

The truck let us off at the junction with the dirt road to Gitagata. I'm back on the road lined with houses and coffee plants. I know everyone who lives here. I want to push open every door and say, "It's me, Mukasonga, I'm back!" and throw myself into their arms in accordance with the long, heartfelt ritual that governs greetings in Rwanda. But I can't. I keep my distance from my sisters as I walk. I try to hide my face. I speed up when I come to my godmother's house. No one must recognize me. It would be dangerous for everyone in Gitagata.

When we get home, my mother bursts into tears, my father can't hide his emotion. But very soon I sense a sort of unease. The door is closed well before nightfall. They listen anxiously for the footsteps of anyone who might be coming to see them. They advise me not to move from the back bedroom. My father speaks in low tones, trying to get something through to me. It's no easy thing to tell a daughter she can't stay with her parents, that she has to be off as soon as she can. This very night. The councilman will end up hearing I've come back, and then Mayor Rwambuka. So . . . They go and fetch Antoine. He will lead Julienne and me back to the border. My joy turns to deep sadness. My mother and I had so much to say to each other, and now we can only weep as we wait for the moment when I have to go. In the middle of the night, we start back to Burundi.

——— ——— ———

I paid my parents one final visit in May 1986. I didn't know it would be the last, of course. This time I wasn't going to Rwanda by secret back ways. I was going with my husband and two children. I was French. The Rwandan embassy at Bujumbura had put a visa in my passport, all according to the rules. I was going home, as a foreigner perhaps, but at least on the main road. And this time I wouldn't be showing up out of the blue. From Butare, my sister Alexia had let my parents know: Mukasonga would be coming to see them, with her husband, with her children, two boys!

On the dirt road to Gitagata, where a vehicle is a rarity, the children ran along behind the car, and when it stopped before the Cosma house, all the neighbors cried, "It's Mukasonga!"

My parents had forgotten their fear for a while. They'd prepared everything needed to celebrate the visit of their daughter, who was bringing them two boys: *ikigage*, sorghum beer, *urwarwa*, banana beer. To add to the splendor of the festivities, they went to buy some Primus from the village shop. I explained to my mother that my husband had been appointed to Djibouti, that I would be going far away, that we might not see each other again for a long time. She was sorry, of course, but at the same time relieved, as if some danger were fading – for them? for me?

Things had changed at my parents': they'd built a new house behind the old hut we'd moved into in 1963. That house was a dream that André, Alexia, and I had sworn to bring about back when we were students: we'd spend our first paychecks as functionaries – because clearly we could be nothing but functionaries – on having a house built for my parents, "a house like the white people's." Oh! not exactly "like the white people's," of course: there was no running water, no electricity, and obviously no bathroom, but there were bedrooms with walls and doors. The whole family had contributed to its construction, with money or labor. For my part, I'd saved up all I could from my modest salary, and I sent them that little sum by way of a Rwandan priest, Father Fulgence, who was an accountant at Caritas Burundi. He forwarded it to Caritas Rwanda, who sent it to the Nyamata parish. I'd done what I could.

But my father had something still more extraordinary to show me. There were cattle in the new yard! My father had managed to put together a new herd. A very meager herd, it's true: three cows and three calves. But my father proudly showed me the bull calf he'd set aside for his grandson, Aurélien, which he would present to him with all the solemnity the occasion requires.

The big party was held the next day. All of Gitagata was there: the men in the yard, the women inside. My father took the floor and, as tradition dictates, sang the praises of his daughter, his son-in-law, and his grandsons, Aurélien and Joël, as well as the little bull he'd reserved for the elder son, Aurélien. One by one, every guest took the floor and was heard out in devout silence as the jugs of beer were handed around, everyone plunging their straws into them. My husband Claude had to make a speech of his own. No one understood it, but they all gravely cheered and applauded.

Among the women, the atmosphere was less solemn. The chatter was interrupted by songs, and we all began to dance. I danced just as I used to at weddings. And in a way my wedding was exactly what my parents wanted to celebrate. The women said, "No one can dance like Mukasonga. There's one who never plays the intellectual, at least." And we reminisced about going to fetch water together, gathering wood, chasing off the monkeys that had come to pillage our sorghum.

Nonetheless, a shadow hung over our joy. A family of strangers appeared at the party, a family my mother had sent someone to go and get. Slightly uncomfortable, my mother quietly explained to me that they were our new neighbors, Hutus from the north of the country. They'd been given a place at the far end of our field. They weren't the only ones. The authorities had assigned lands to families from Ruhengeri and Gisenyi. Those provinces were overcrowded, it's true, but above all the Habyarimana regime was depending on their support. Nyamata was now teeming with faithful supporters of the president. "You understand," my mother explained, "there was nothing else I could do. We had to invite them. For one thing, they're our neighbors. And they would have found out anyway."

I shared the beer with them. In the yard, their children ate alongside the others. They were still living at the end of our field in 1994. What did they see? What did they do?

Our plan was to spend several days in Nyamata. But the next day my mother came to tell me discreetly that it would be best if we left: "It's better for the children," she said as a pretext, "they're not used to our food." I understood: my children and I might be in danger, but above all our presence was a menace for my parents, and for the whole family.

———

The next day we set off on the road to Burundi again. I can still see my mother, on the edge of the dirt road, her slight form wrapped in her *pagne*. That's the last image I have of her, a little silhouette disappearing at the bend in the road.

1994: The genocide, the long-awaited horror

Anguish overcomes me when I think of that spring of 1994. I still find myself wondering how I could have gone on tending to my house and children, taking courses for certification as a social worker in France, admiring the flowering trees of that French springtime. I sleepwalked my way through those months of April, May, and June. I knew there was no hope for Nyamata. As early as March 1992, there'd been a dress rehearsal in Bugesera: houses were burned, Tutsis were thrown into the latrines. Antonia Locatelli, an Italian volunteer, was murdered for trying to alert the international press. My family escaped the slaughter that time, but for how long? My father sent me a letter. Strangely emphatic, he wrote that it was raining as he'd never seen it rain before. The message wasn't hard to decode. The Tutsis of Nyamata were waiting for the holocaust. How could they have escaped it?

It was Habyarimana's death that set off what everyone in Nyamata knew was coming, something that would be named by a word I'd never heard before: genocide. In Kinyarwanda, we would call it *gutsembatsemba*, a verb that means something like "to eradicate," formerly used to talk about rabid dogs or destructive animals. When I learned of the first massacres, immediately after Habyarimana's death, it was like a brief moment of deliverance: at last! Now we could stop living our lives waiting for death to come. It was there. There was no way to escape it. The Tutsis' fated destiny would be fulfilled. A morbid satisfaction flashed through my mind: we in Nyamata had so long expected this! But how could I have conceived the depth of the horror that would overtake Rwanda? An entire people engaged in the most unthinkable crimes, against old people, women, children, babies, with a cruelty and a ferocity so inhuman that even today the killers feel no remorse.

I was not with my family when they were being hacked up with machetes. How could I have simply gone on living my life, as they were all dying? Survival! That was the mission our parents had assigned André and me, it's true. We were supposed to survive, and now I knew what the sorrow of survival meant. It was an enormous weight landing on my shoulders, a very real weight that kept me from climbing the little staircase to the classroom, that paralyzed me at my apartment's front door, unable to open it and step through. I was burdened with the memory of all those dead: they would be with me for as long as I lived.

We in Nyamata had long since accepted that death would be our only deliverance. We waited for it, watched for it, inventing and reinventing ways to escape it all the same – until the next time, when it would come even closer, when it would carry off neighbors, schoolmates, brothers, a son. And mothers trembled with horror when they gave birth to a boy, because he would be an Inyenzi, and anyone who pleased could humiliate him, hunt him down, murder him, and they'd never be punished. We were tired; sometimes we gave in to the longing to die. Yes, we were prepared to face death, but not a death that was forced on us. We were Inyenzi, fit only to be crushed like cockroaches, with one stomp. But they preferred to watch us die slowly. They drew out the death throes with unspeakable tortures, purely for their own pleasure. They liked to cut up their victims while they were still living, they liked to disembowel the women and rip out their fetuses. And that pleasure I cannot forgive. It will be with me forever, like a vile heartless laugh.

André and I could only call the roll of our dead:

> my father Cosma, 79 years old;
> my mother Stefania, maybe 74;
> my older sister Judith, her four children, and I'm no

longer sure how many grandchildren;

   my brother Antoine and his wife, with nine children, the oldest twenty, the youngest five;

   Alexia and her husband Pierre Ntereye, and four of their children, between two and ten years of age;

   Jeanne, my younger sister, her four children, Douce, eight, Nella, seven, Christian, five, Nénette, one, and the baby she was eight months pregnant with.

I counted them up over and over again. There were thirty-seven.

I already knew their remains would never be found. Now there's no doubt. Were they picked up by the schoolchildren who spent and still spend their vacations gathering bones on the hills and in the fields, to be deposited in the crypt beneath the church of Nyamata? Bones and skulls that will be nameless forever, piled behind the glass walls of the ossuary. Or were their corpses devoured and scattered by the packs of masterless dogs that roamed Bugesera in the months after the genocide? Are they still buried deep in one of those mass graves that are forever being discovered?

   Where are they? Somewhere deep in the anonymous crowd of the genocide's victims. A million of them, their lives stolen, their names lost. What's the point of counting up our dead again and again? From the thousand hills of Rwanda, a million shades answer my call.

There were survivors, of course. No genocide is perfect. In May, I began trying to locate people who might have been spared. I harassed the Rwandan diaspora, the Red Cross, Doctors Without Borders, and many other NGOs with desperate phone calls. I even wrote Bernard Kouchner. I wasn't thinking anymore. I was acting, like a robot. I wrote a long letter to Danielle Mitterand. I was advised not to send it.

Everyone was talking about unaccompanied minors. It was a fashionable phrase. Some of our children might have been among them. Even in Nyamata, there might still have been a few orphans left. They were my children too. It was for their sake that I joined with the other students from the social work school, my professors, and many friends, to found an association. We did our best to collect money so we could come to their aid once contact was restored.

It wasn't until November that I learned Alexia and Pierre Ntereye's two daughters, Jeanne-Françoise, fourteen, and Rita, six, had been found. My brother had come from Senegal to get them. He was the oldest, and now he was the head of the family; it was his duty to take them in, just as if they were his own children. I did what I could to help him pay for the trip. Later still, I heard that Jeanne's husband Emmanuel had also been spared. He'd found one of his daughters, Emmanuella, three years old, whom we all called Nana. Finally there was Jocelyne, one of Judith's daughters. Her husband and child had been killed. She'd been raped. She was pregnant by one of her killers. They'd forgotten to kill her, unless they had a slower death in mind: they'd given her AIDS.

All I have of my loved ones' deaths are black holes and fragments of horror. What hurts the worst? Not knowing how they died or knowing how they were killed? The fear they felt, the cruelty they endured, sometimes it seems I now have to endure it in turn, flee it in turn. All I have left is the terrible guilt of living on amid so many dead. But what is my pain next to everything they suffered before their tormentors granted them the death that was their only escape?

In February 1995 I went to Thiès, in Senegal, to see my brother André, who'd just brought our nieces home with him. I hadn't come to hear their story, I only wanted to be by their side, to hold them close, as if that could still mean anything to them, to weep with them, if they could weep. I'm not sure if it was someone who'd lived through the Shoah or the Tutsi massacres who said that a genocide survivor is in reality a "sub-vivor". That's exactly how it was. Jeanne-Françoise and her little sister were sub-vivors. They survived, but they weren't alive, they were outside of themselves, oblivious to their own existence, without family in the midst of their relatives, of cousins their own age, in a becalmed, frozen present, an unspeakable past that came back only in their nightmares, a future with no future. How long did that last? It took my brother's courage, his wife Clotilde's endless patience, the cousins' happy, thoughtful kindness, it took all that for Jeanne-Françoise and Rita to recover a little of their taste for a life they'd been driven out of. Now, back in Rwanda, they are beautiful, vital young girls. That makes me proud. And it would be a victory without bitterness if their parents and their brothers could share in their laughter. But often I have doubts: could that will to survive be only a remission? Neither André nor I nor anyone else can claim to be sure that scars are all that remains of their wounds. Can we hope that their future will be a kinder one?

——— ——— ———

On the other hand, I did end up hearing the story of the cruel deaths of my brother-in-law Pierre Ntereye, my sister Alexia, and their sons. Pierre was a university professor. No doubt entirely against his wishes, he'd been helped along in his career – one of the few Tutsis the government favored to show naïve or complicit Europeans that ethnic discrimination was unknown in Hutu-run Rwanda. He must have seemed a perfect fit for the part: he had what was considered a Tutsi physique, his clan always held the highest ranks back in the days of the monarchy. They'd allowed him to study in Belgium and the United States. Jeanne-Françoise, his oldest daughter, was born in Mons. Of course, he was forbidden the political career his Hutu fellow students had already charted out for themselves, but he would still be a university professor, in Butare and then in Ruhengeri. Pierre was no dupe, he knew perfectly well they were using him, but did he have any choice? He would pay dearly for the ambiguous favors the regime had done him.

Sensing a threat, Pierre had taken his family to Taba, in the Gitarama province, his homeland, convinced they'd be safer there. The mayor of Taba was Jean-Paul Akayesu, later tried and found guilty by the International Criminal Tribunal in Arusha. He was a friend of the Ntereye family. He'd promised to protect Pierre. The fury of the genocide soon swept away that friendship and those promises.

They came to arrest him, and Pierre gravely injured himself as he was trying to flee. Rather than let him die, his tormentors gave him medical treatment so they could torture him at their leisure. They kept him prisoner in the town hall. For the next several days, they cut pieces off of him one by one with a machete.

Jeanne-Françoise saw her father being slowly dismembered. She didn't make a moving story out of it. I heard her speak only a few sentences, as if ripped from an incurable sorrow. I never tried to bring them out. She comes to me: "Auntie, I have something to tell you." In a detached tone, she begins to tell. But suddenly the story breaks off. Her head hurts. Everything's gone blurry. She feels dizzy. She wants to be left alone. She closes herself up in a pain that can never be soothed.

In Rwanda, it's the families who bring prisoners their food. That was what Jeanne-Françoise did. It must have been pure sadism on the part of the jailors. Every day, then, Jeanne-Françoise had to bring her father his meal, and every day she saw him with another piece gone: fingers, a hand, an arm, a leg. She had to stand before the blood-spattered shreds that were once the father she was so proud of, the father she describes as so handsome, so strong, so intelligent. It was that very idea of her father they'd set out to destroy, replacing it with the unspeakable image of a rag of bleeding flesh, forcing that image upon her, forcing her to accept that this was her father.

Her four little brothers were also killed in the town hall. Alexia was executed not long before the arrival of the Rwandan Patriotic Army. All the witnesses regret that the liberation came just a little too late for her. They also say the killers had Alexia choose her own burial place. There were three left: perhaps reserved for her and her daughters. That was what they did with high-status victims.

After the death of their mother and four brothers, Jeanne-Fran-çoise and Rita were taken in by an aunt who was married to a Hutu. A very precarious sanctuary, because some of the cousins were against having them there, while others wanted to protect them. In the end, with the complicity of the aunt, one of the cousins took them to a safer hiding place, far from Taba, on his bicycle. I tried to learn more about that hiding place, but whenever Jeanne-Françoise speaks of that time, she breaks off, says she has a bad headache, walls herself up in an impregnable silence. The two sisters later went back to their aunt's house in Taba, and for several months those two pam-pered city girls lived the hard life so well-known to peasant women. Then my brother André came to take them to Senegal, awaiting the day when his family, which now included the two orphans, would return to Rwanda for good.

——— ——— ———

Now I have to talk about Jeanne. I've been dreading this moment for a long time. There were five girls and two boys in my family; Jeanne was the youngest, maybe the one I was closest to. I was her "little mother," as we say. I carried her on my back. She followed me everywhere. We tried to look like each other. People said she might almost be my twin. When she was born, the whole family greeted her like a gift fallen from heaven: a very black, very happy little baby. I want to keep Jeanne's smile in my memory like the most precious of all treasures.

Her husband Emmanuel told me how she died. He said he owed it to me. He'd never spoken of it to anyone before. I recorded his words. What he wanted to tell me he would probably never say again. It was very hard for both of us. I thought of telling him to stop, to put an end to the pain his story was reawakening. He wanted to go on to the end. But he didn't tell me everything. The most unthinkable horror he couldn't bring himself to say, or perhaps he was trying to spare me. But that part I already knew: my niece Jocelyne had sent me a strange letter, almost illegible, but readable enough to tell me what I never should have known.

I wish I could write this page with my tears.

———

Emmanuel's roots were in Ruhengeri. His family was among the deportees in Gitagata, where he was a teacher. But the young couple and their children retreated to the village of Nyamata after the 1992 massacres. On April 6th, at around 8:30 pm, Habyarimana's plane is shot down. On the 7th, a curfew is imposed in Nyamata and throughout Rwanda, but, even closed up in their house all day long, Emmanuel and Jeanne sense a great agitation, which is encouraged by the subprefect Hassan Djuma and the mayor Bernard Gatanazi. On Friday the 8th, the first escapees reach Nyamata from the neighboring Kibungo and Kanzenze sectors, where the genocide began on the 7th. At 7:30 in the evening, a grenade is thrown at the house. The windows shatter, but no one is hurt. The family seeks refuge at a neighbor's. The locals organize night patrols to sound the alert in case of danger, but soldiers quickly intervene and order everyone back in their houses. As they disperse, two men are shot and left for dead. Toward 1:30 in the morning, a second grenade is thrown at Emmanuel and Jeanne's now-empty house, slightly damaging the roof.

On the 9th, the people are summoned to what is announced as a "pacification meeting." Artillery fire can be heard in the distance, toward Kigali. The subprefect seizes on that sound to stir up the Hutu population: "Do you hear that? They want to kill us all."

The situation is growing more critical by the minute, so Emmanuel and his neighbor decide to take their families to Kayumba Hill, overlooking Nyamata. Many Tutsis have already taken shelter there, trying to organize resistance. Emmanuel comes back to Nyamata and hides. On Sunday he climbs back up to Kayumba. "And that," he says, "was the last I ever saw of Jeanne and my children."

On Monday the 11th, the soldiers and a mob of volunteer killers launch an assault on Kayumba. The Tutsi families flee for the church in Nyamata. There they will be massacred on the 14th, five to six thousand of them. The day before, soldiers from the UN peacekeeping force, the UNAMIR, had come to evacuate the white nuns and missionaries.

Jeanne is eight months pregnant and in no condition to flee with the terrified crowd. She entrusts her three oldest children to her neighbors as they set off for Nyamata with the rest. She's been wounded by a machete. She hides in a bush and stays there with Nana, her youngest child. How long does she go on hiding there? No one can tell me. Unable to bear staying there any longer, knowing nothing of her children's fate, she decides to start back down for Nyamata. She will be killed in front of the town hall. How? By whom? Jocelyn's letter is as precise and as incoherent as a nightmare. Wounded, Jeanne falls to the ground. Her belly is sliced open. The fetus is ripped out. They beat her with the fetus. Nana is at her side. The killers go on their way, leaving Nana there with her. And then someone, and I will never know who that someone is, asks a dying Jeanne, as she lies in a pool of her own blood, what he can do for her. "You can't do anything for me, but if you can do something, take Nana with you."

I don't need to unfold the sheet of notebook paper lying before me. Jocelyne's words parade through my head. The words are emotionless, made cold by death. They come from the land of the dead.

Emmanuel is among the last of the survivors hiding in the swamps. For forty days, he manages to elude the killers' daily hunts. On the 14th of May, the Rwandan Patriotic Army liberates Nyamata. Of the sixty thousand Tutsis recorded in the municipality of Nyamata in January 1994, there remain only five thousand survivors – 5,348, to be precise. The Rwandan Patriotic Front sets up a temporary administration. Serving as mayor is a woman, a Hutu, whose Tutsi husband has been killed. The survivors struggle to find their way back to some kind of life.

Toward the end of May, he's no longer sure of the date, Emmanuel was in Kibari, not far from the Rwakibirizi spring, to help the son of Gitagata's tailor Berkimasse pull his father's body from the latrines where the killers had thrown it. "There," he says, "someone came to tell me he'd heard a man from Musenyi saying all sorts of things, and one of them was that he'd found a little girl on the road, a girl named Nana. They took me to see him, and he confirmed that the little girl had said again and again that her mother was called Jeanne and her father Emmanuel. The RPF soldiers had taken her away, he didn't know where. The RPF soldiers were gathering lost children in a camp they'd established in a former orphanage in Nyamata. They were looking for teachers among the survivors, to look after the children until the schools reopened. I went to the camp and Nana was there. A captain of the Patriotic Army had found her and grown fond of her. But, since the liberation offensive was still advancing, he had to leave her at the improvised orphanage. I was so physically and mentally exhausted, and Nana was so little and fragile, that for the moment I thought it was best to leave her with a friend, Marie-Louise, who'd lost her whole family too. Nana would have a little motherly warmth again, and Marie-Louise would have a child to give some sense to her survival. I took Nana back when her school reopened. Nana learned to smile again, and her smile fills me with joy and sadness: isn't that Jeanne's smile, and the smile of all our lost children?"

2004: On the trail of the land of the dead

Emmanuel, my children, my husband, and I sit crammed inside a pickup truck from the school as it slowly drives down Nyamata's main street, dodging the potholes. Under the few shops' corrugated metal awnings I see piled-up sacks of rice and beans, cases of beer, Fanta . . . The market is set up at the side of the street, on a huge rectangular lot. Further on, minibuses are waiting for travelers going to Kigali; others are lined up at the only gas pump, run by a solidly-built old man. I try in vain to recognize some face in the crowd, as if I were hoping those who are no more might suddenly appear before me. Like a shipwrecked sailor clinging to a broken mast, I keep my eyes fixed on the comforting sight of the old colonial houses that were once home to Gatashya, the veterinarian, and Bitega, who ran the infirmary. I'm glad to see that the little woods of Gatigisimu, where we used to relieve ourselves before class, is still there. Slowly we drive out of the village. A few last houses, surrounded by neatly trimmed euphorbia hedges, and then the dusty road goes on toward a vast, flat horizon: this isn't the land of a thousand hills, this is Bugesera!

The truck drives by little groups of women with baskets of beans or sweet potatoes on their heads. It slows down to pass zigzagging bicycles loaded with green bananas. I wish it would slow down still more. I know that, a few kilometers further on, we'll reach the spot where a little dirt road forks off to the right. For ten years I've been dreading this moment, doing everything I could to put it off. The truck will turn right onto the little dirt road no one ever takes anymore, the road to Gitwe, to Gitagata, to Cyohoha, the road that leads to those who are no more.

It was a long time before I could bring myself to go back to Rwanda after the genocide. A very long time. I couldn't find the strength. Rwandan refugees in France were going home. That was their duty. Rwanda had to be rebuilt. Rwandan women married to French men, as I was, were hurrying back to hold a surviving father, mother, brother, or sister in their arms. But what reason did I have for going back to Nyamata? There was no father, no mother, no brother, no sister. André couldn't find so much as a trace of their houses. There was nothing in Gitagata but overgrown cassava bushes and dying banana trees, slowly being smothered by brambles. Where would I go to reflect and remember? Who would share my grief? I was afraid I might show my nieces not the power of hope but only the pain that inhabited me. Would my tears not revive their sobs? And mixed up with their faces, was it not the faces of my parents, of my brother and sisters, that I wanted to hold in my hands? I had to wait, recover the strength I'd never lacked until then. This was why I threw all my energy into the association I'd founded. Helping the resettled orphans. Supporting the reopening of the schools, equipping the junior high school created in 1986 by the parents' association of Nyamata so their children could go on with their studies in spite of the discrimination. I continually put off my departure. The tickets were too expensive, I told myself, that money was better spent on the orphans. Then I went right back to planning a trip: again and again, I set a date, then put it off for one more year. Ten years went by that way. A bad feeling was growing inside me, and I knew that one day I'd have to go back to Nyamata, that I was being called there by the living and the dead alike.

For the past few days, I've been in a Rwanda I thought I'd never know. It's my country, as it is every other Rwandan's. I don't have to walk with my head down, I don't jump at the sight of a uniform. There are no roadblocks where my "ethnic group" will be checked. I won't be humiliated by the militia. I'm not an Inyenzi anymore.

My nose isn't too long, my hair isn't Ethiopian: I'm a Rwandan. I'm eager to discover the Rwanda forbidden to me before. I want to see everything: Gikongoro, where I was born, on the banks of the river Rukarara, and Lake Kivu, Kibuye, Ruhengeri, Gisenyi, the volcanoes . . . I wish the minibus would stop at every bend in the road to let the hills and mountaintops all the way to the horizon come and fill my eyes. Again and again – the others gently poke fun at me for it – I say, *"Rwanda nziza, Rwanda nziza*: My country is beautiful."

But Rwanda is also the land of tears, and the roads we travel take us on a long journey through horror and grief.

Here are the classrooms in Murambi, where hundreds of skeletons remain frozen in their last terrified pose, or broken by the torture they endured. The guard lost his entire family. He hoists up the huge pounder used to crush babies' skulls. He points out the circle of stones where a flagpole once stood. The French soldiers raised their flag on that pole; it fluttered over the mass graves, hastily covered up. The school sits on a plateau, and beyond it we can see a vast circle of hills. Night is falling. Smoke rises peacefully from huts half hidden in the banana groves. Who could ever believe it in this gentle twilight? The killers are still there.

From Magi, the place my family was expelled from in 1960, we follow the mountaintops overlooking the Kanyaru. The churches are places of worship again, but the scars left by bullets and grenades bear witness to what happened there. The survivor friend who's guiding us explains that in this riverside region the Tutsis weren't actually killed in the churches; they were hunted down and herded into them, then driven along by dogs and machine-gun fire to the Kanyaru, to drown.

Our friend takes us to his parents' house. He was lucky. His parents were too old; they weren't driven to the river but killed in their yard. He was able to locate their bodies. He buried them by the front door to the church in Kirarambogo, where his father had been a teacher for twenty-five years. His former students, who are also the killers, pass by his grave when they go to Sunday Mass like good Christians.

In Mbazi, near Butare, we stop at a large rectangle of cement. No inscription. No name. At the bottom of a nearby valley, our friend explains, Tutsis were massacred with machine guns: sixty-five thousand of them. Dried bouquets lie strewn in the dirt all around the slab. We ask the children attracted by the car what happened, why the flowers are no longer on the grave. "It was a crazy woman," they answer after a moment's hesitation. "It was a crazy woman who did that." Since we take our time about leaving, they put the bouquets back on the concrete.

Rare are the survivors who could find their loved ones' remains and bury them in a grave. And in any case, however others may envy it, that privilege isn't necessarily helpful for the "grief work" psychologists talk about. A friend tells me how she found her parents' corpses:

"Long after the genocide, I went back to my parents' yard, in Gahanga. I was with a young man my parents had adopted, who'd somehow escaped the massacre. He'd seen everything. He guided me through the scene of the slaughter. All I could think of was finding my parents' bodies. We questioned a Hutu who was living there. Needless to say, he didn't know anything, he hadn't seen anything, he hadn't done anything, he wasn't there . . . I carefully explained that I wasn't accusing him, I was looking for my parents' bodies, not their killer. That wasn't enough to earn his trust. But I refused to be discouraged: I kept at it for the next several days. In the end, I offered him money. That he couldn't resist. He gave in and took me a few kilometers away, where he showed me a ditch my parents had been thrown into.

"There were many formalities to go through for permission to bury my parents in their yard. In the end, I got it. I was proud of my victory: I was bringing my parents back, now they could rest in their yard. I had my parents all to myself, I could weep over their grave, put flowers on it. I told myself again and again, 'Now they're home, thanks to me.' And I'd found a reason for surviving: so I could go to Gahanga and my parents' grave.

"But it didn't last. As time went by, I dreaded going to their grave more and more. I came up with excuse after excuse to put off my self-imposed pilgrimage. I didn't like being alone at their grave. I couldn't bear mourning for them on my own. That feeling paralyzed me, and for a long time I tried to fight it off, but in the end I didn't want to abandon my parents, I was afraid they'd be left all alone in their yard in Gahanga. I had them exhumed and taken to Rebero, in Kigali, to be put in the Memorial, with all the others. Now I can weep with the childless mothers, the widows, the widowers, the orphans. It's as if I were sharing their suffering, as if they were all helping me bear my pain. I might have found my place on the long road of mourning we have to follow. I'm not sure yet . . . "

But many survivors have no choice but to wander aimlessly on death's shores. There are fewer than ten of them left in Murambi. They had to leave their enclosures in the hills, and they gathered in the makeshift village around the market. They couldn't go on living among their killers, amid the stares that said all too clearly that they weren't supposed to be there. They expect nothing from the Gacaca courts, the justice handed down by the wise men of the hills. In Murambi, they say that the "wise men" named to the court will unavoidably have blood on their hands. They hope it won't be their children's, at least. "I myself," one told me, "I tried to make a new life. I remarried. I had a son. When he was old enough for school they took him from me and killed him. That's what the Hutus are telling us: there's no place for the Tutsis on this earth. So I became a guard at the Memorial. This is the only place I can feel at home, with the bones. I feel safe in the company of the dead. Here with the skeletons, this is where I belong. It's hard for me to leave them when the Memorial closes for the day, hard to go back to the living, to people pretending to be living. So we survivors stick close together, in silence. Everywhere around us, on the hills, our killers are lighting their lamps, and we're alone in the darkness. You're a Tutsi like me, but still, you live abroad, you can't really understand us – not even people from Kigali can understand everything. You can't feel the fear that comes over us, that chills us to the bone. No night is darker and longer than night in Murambi."

——— ——— ———

Now we've reached the junction with the dirt road to Gitagata. The dry-season landscape feels like a barren steppe, dry and dusty. And yet people once lived here. On the right, just where the dirt road meets the highway to Gako, that was Rwabashi's house. He was a privileged one, Rwabashi. No one knows why, but two of his sons were allowed to stay "in Rwanda." They must have had good jobs there, because their parents didn't have to farm. They hired people to work in their fields. All day long Rwabashi sat in front of his house, draped in his white *pagne*, with his tall silvery hair, holding his stick very straight. He greeted people as they passed. His wife Isabelle waited for callers. Everyone admired and envied her. She seemed to live far above the misery and fear felt by the rest of us. Women visited her in hopes her insouciance would rub off on them. Being with her, they could take heart: there was at least one person who seemed utterly unaware of the torment that had come to us.

———

Candida and I often stopped by Rwabashi's on the way home from school. His daughter Tatiana would give us something to drink, and sometimes to eat. That helped us on our way up the big hill to Gitwe, and often it was our only meal of the day.

Ex-sub-chief Ruvebana's hut was across the road. He didn't stay long. He couldn't come home after the events of Christmas 1963. He was a wanted man, and his life was in danger. He hid in the bush, on Rebero Hill, behind his house. My father secretly brought him food. Then he left for Burundi, and we never saw him again. Separated from her son for the first time, his mother Suzanne slowly died of grief. That separation also deeply affected my father, even if he never let it show. His boss was also his friend and confidant, and writing him was out of the question, since any correspondence with an Inyenzi in Burundi was considered a crime.

A little past the junction, the driver turns off the road and into the bush. We stop at the foot of a hill. This is Rebero. The slope isn't particularly steep on this side. The ground is strewn with loose stones, white and rust-red, and the half-buried boulders fall into thin, sharp-edged shards. There's a little eucalyptus grove at the top. From there, you can see all of Bugesera. Nyamata and the valley of the Nyabarongo are behind us, hidden between two mountain ridges. In front of us, the very straight road leading to Gako and the Burundi border. On the right, the lake where I used to fetch water is now only a papyrus swamp. Gakindo and Rukindo hills lie beyond it, and behind them is Lake Cyohoha South, gleaming in the sun. The municipalities – today the districts – of Gashora and Ngenda are laid out at our feet like a relief map. I recognize the tile roofs of the Mayange market shops in Gashora, and the Ruhuha market in Ngenda. Not far away are the colonial buildings of the Karama Agricultural Institute. Well before the horizon, the hills just visible in the haze are already Burundi.

It was on Rebero Hill that most of the inhabitants of Gitwe, Gitagata, and Cyohoha gathered to defend themselves from the murderous mob. That came on the 11th, 12th, and 13th of April. Philibert, one of Froduald's sons, told me the story. He was ten years old at the time. The massacres began in the villages on the 11th, and everyone saw at once that these weren't the usual revenge killings. This was an outright extermination, and no one would be spared, not women, not children, not the elderly. Everyone who was healthy and mobile fled to Rebero. The rest – old or ill or too weak to struggle for survival – stayed and waited for the killers to come. They didn't have to wait long . . . For two days, the people who'd got to Rebero held off their attackers. Once they'd built the women and children a shelter among the eucalyptus trees, the men took up sharp Rebero stones to fight back their killers' machetes. Unable to manage on their own, the Interahamwe militia and Hutu mobs from Gashora and Ngenda asked the soldiers from Gako for help; the soldiers sprayed the hill with fragmentation grenades, and then the hordes of ordinary killers finished the job with machetes. That was on the 13th of April. Froduald and his family were killed, but Philibert and one of his brothers escaped the slaughter, buried beneath a pile of corpses. Philibert assures me that Antoine was there, with his entire family. That's where they were killed, all eleven of them. My older sister Judith's whole extended family was there too, and most of her children. But not my parents. Philibert knew them well. We were neighbors, and since Froduald was Antoine's best friend and had risked his life for us, he was considered one of the family. My parents were too old to seek shelter on Rebero; it was hard for them to get around. And I think, too, that after more than thirty years they were tired of being persecuted and pursued: why bother struggling to survive once again? I imagine, but I will never know, that they waited in their house, waiting for death to come.

No memorial has been built on Rebero. Nothing to commemorate the fallen but boulders and white and rust-red stones. I look for signs from the hill, I dig at the ground. The sun is straight overhead. This is the hour of mirages. I push away the little rocks, I scratch at the ground. I find a shred of tattered cloth half-buried in the dirt. I try to convince myself that it comes from Antoine's shirt. I hesitate, then leave that false relic where it lies. I pick up a stone with a sharp edge. In remembrance.

——— ——— ———

We've gone back to the dirt road. The truck is climbing the hillside toward Gitwe. Between the erosion and the creeping undergrowth, the road is hard to make out. But our driver Paulin is a survivor from Gitagata, and he knows the way.

Now we're crossing through what was once Gitwe – what we called the Abafundo neighborhood, to be precise. The Abafundo were families with roots in Gikongoro. They were proud people. Their sons would only marry Abafundo women, whom they looked for among the refugees deported to the Rubago camp, in Gisaka. There were ten houses, lined up on either side of the dirt road.

The first one, on the left, belonged to the schoolteacher Birota. He wasn't an Umufundo. He came later, and moved into a house left empty by a family who'd fled to Burundi. He, the intellectual, was critized for marrying his daughter Uwamariya into a family of pagans who couldn't read or write, but who owned cows, the only ones left who did. People said he'd traded his daughter for milk.

A little further on lived Gahutu. His name, "the little Hutu," made everyone laugh, because his size and his ways were straight from a caricature of a Tutsi. And, people joked, that name hadn't even done him any good! His wife Karuyonga was tall and heavy and always in a sunny mood. Everyone agreed that she was made to have a big family, so she was pitied for having brought only four children into the world: Rugema, Rubare, Maria, and the oldest sister, who'd stayed behind "in Rwanda." Everyone wished her courage, because for us a real family began with seven children. Rubare was admired for his bowed legs, an unmistakable sign of nobility! I sometimes spent nights at Maria's. There was also her aunt, Mukarurangwa. The two girls were more or less the same age, and I was still little. As custom dictates, the family had built them a straw hut in the yard. We sang, we danced around a jug of sorghum beer. I liked sleeping at Maria's.

There was also my godmother Angelina's house. Her husband Nyagatare was a teacher. He'd opened the first school in Gitwe. They had just one daughter, Clotilde, who was killed in Butare, but their house was always full of children. The children of the poorest families were always welcome there, and she'd adopted several orphans from her own family, massacred at Gikongoro. Angelina seemed to me the epitome of progress and elegance. Even the food we ate at her house had the taste of modernity: there was sauce!

Bihara lived across the road from my godmother with his wife Steria and his six children. One of the daughters, Bernadette, was with me at Notre-Dame-de-Cîteaux. She was a great friend of my sister Alexia. Their husbands became university professors, colleagues, and friends. I found two surviving brothers from that family in Nyamata. Twenty years after, we recognized each other without a moment's hesitation. They said they'd been lucky. At least they weren't alone: "There are two of us sharing our sorrow," says Rutayisire, holding his brother in his arms, his eyes damp with tears. "That's all we have left to share."

But how, beneath the acacias and the brush, to make out the houses of those who once lived there, whose very memory the killers tried to erase: Musonera, Rugema, Musoni, Muganga, Costasia, Karamage, and the faces of all their children, which haunt my memory alone?

With Gashumba's house began the neighborhood of the deportees from Butare. On the left, leading up to the primary school, there were six houses: they belonged to Gashumba, Ruhaya, Kiguru, Ruhurura, Harukwandiye, and Rugereka, who was actually from Byumba. No one lived across the road from them. They'd all fled to Burundi in 1963.

Ruhaya was a Hutu who'd faithfully followed his chief into exile. He was treated with particular cruelty by the soldiers, even more than we were. When they made everyone line up along the dirt road, Ruhaya protested that he was a Hutu and started back to his work. The soldiers then asked what he was doing among the Tutsis, and they laughed as they beat him.

Ruhurura moved into our first house after we left it. He was a former chief who'd fallen into the deepest poverty. His first wife had left him and gone off to Kigali. He then lived with a simple peasant woman, relying on her to do the farming, but their land went untended, and the house was disturbingly run-down. We all felt sorry for their children: little skeletons, half-eaten by chigoe fleas.

Just by the school lived Kagango, the father of Régis, who was killed at the Kabgayi seminary in 1973. Kagango was an artist and a healer. He sculpted canes. People came from far away to buy them. He didn't need to farm, particularly because along with his talents as a sculptor he had a more mysterious gift: with a mere touch of his fingers, he could heal sprains and twisted ankles. We looked with fascination at his hands, whose palms were strangely white, and seemed to be covered with scales, like a lizard.

There's no school in Gitwe nowadays, of course, since there are no children, and the *iminazi*, the tall trees that so generously dropped their fruit on our slates, have all disappeared.

Nor is there any trace of the village's last twelve houses, two facing rows of six. I call out to a little boy herding goats, who has appeared out of nowhere. He might be eight or nine years old. His goats are feeding on the sparse bramble bushes, and I say to him, "Do you know that there used to be children right there where your goats are eating?" Terrified, the child flees with his herd in a little cloud of dust. This evening he'll say to his mother, "Mama, I met a crazy woman on the old road." And his mother will be angry and tell him, "Never go there again. That's the land of the dead." And meanwhile I recite the names of all those who have no one left to mourn them. I cry out their names – to whom? for whom?

Théodore, the teacher.

Rutabana, whose rice I so loved.

Rukorera, the man who had cows. He and his family were pagans, and the children didn't go to school. But he was envied: he had cows, and many sons. In exchange for a little milk, Rukorera could always find volunteers to work in his fields. His cows had the right to graze anywhere they liked. In return, he gave away manure to fertilize the fields or warm cow urine to treat the children's intestinal worms.

Buregeya, who thought himself handsome, and who'd married Mariya, universally considered one of the village's most beautiful girls.

Tadeyo Nshimiyimana, who was greatly respected, as he was a fifth-grade teacher at the big school in Nyamata.

His mother Yosefa, whose sons had all gone off to study. One of them, Matayo, had come back to Nyamata. He used to wander the bush to study the birds. He wrote down their songs in a notebook. He only spoke to himself, always in French or Latin. Everyone made fun of him, they called him the mad scientist, but they were also a little afraid of him.

Édouard Sebucocera, a close friend of my father; it was to them that the people from Butare turned when there were serious decisions to be made.

And then François Seburyumunyu, Kabarari, and his two brothers Mujinja and Karara, and Inyansi, the only adult deported in 1960 who was still living.

In the next house lived Sekimonyo, the beekeeper. He was always looking for trees for his hives. People said the good Lord had made him for that trade, because he was so tall he could easily reach the highest branches.

The last one on the row, Maguge's house, sat at the edge of the forest that separated Gitwe from Gitagata. His wife was named Kiragi, which means "the deaf woman," and she was indeed deaf and dumb. A mystery hung over the death of his first wife. All of that made Maguge a disturbing figure, particularly because he always wore a big black hat that frightened the children. They called him Kiroko, the ogre.

Gihanga, considered lucky because one of his daughters, Emma Mariya, had married Bahima, a rich merchant in Nyamata. She'd raised some ten children. They were all killed, like her.

——— ——— ———

Between Gitwe and Gitagata there was a little stretch of brush, now no different from the places people once lived. But as soon as the dirt road begins to descend toward the swampy lowland that was once Lake Cyohoha North – for the lake too has disappeared – I know we're on Pétronille's grounds: this is Gitagata. I look for the big fig tree that marked the entrance to the village: yes, it's still there, but it's lost all its leaves, it's a towering skeleton of dead wood, yet another. The road runs along tall, dark-green hedges, like giant funeral hangings: the old enclosures' euphorbia plants, now wild and overgrown. Behind them is a tangle of brambles, as if no human being had ever ventured that far. And yet men, women, and children once lived in this place, even if the right to live was denied them, even if no effort was spared to erase every trace of their existence. And when I close my eyes, what I see is always the same night, a night in the dry season, a night lit by the full moon. The women are busy around the three stones of the hearth. Sitting cross-legged on either side of the road, the men are gravely talking and passing around calabashes of sorghum or banana beer. Little boys are playing with a banana-leaf ball in the road; others are racing after the old bicycle wheels they use as hoops, giggling wildly. The girls have swept the yard and the road, and now they're singing and dancing. And now the women are studying the moon, whose illuminated face, they believe, reveals the future. In my memories, that enormous moon is always there, hanging over the village to pour out its pale blue light.

In the bright night of my memory, they're all there.

Sindabye, one of whose daughters, Valérie, was at the School of Social Work in Butare, in the auxiliary program.

Rwahinyuza: he had a son, Claudiyani, who became a shopkeeper in Nyamata. He was the only one who owned a car. He did favors for everyone. People called on him to transport the sick.

Tito's widow Felicita, who had no choice but to farm all alone to feed the two children she was left with. But everyone in Gitwe and Gitagata gave her their help. She was the village widow.

Donati, Mariya's brother. He worked at the Karama Agricultural Institute, and came to Gitagata only to liven up wedding parties, because he was the best dancer. He was considered as good-looking as his sister, and he himself was convinced it was true.

And then there were two girls who lived alone with their invalid mother: Bwanakeye and Runura, who had a limp. They had no way to defend themselves from the young men of the Party, who made playthings of them.

So many others vie for space in my memories: Suzanne, the aged Nyiragasheshe, Athanase, Gashugi, Theresa, Godeliva, Nteri's widow, Nyirarwenga, Siridiyo . . .

——— ——— ———

In the bush, now brown with the dry season, what was once Antoine's yard is easy to make out. It's the only one with big trees whose leaves are still green, looking strangely exotic amid the thorny undergrowth. He planted them with the seeds he brought home from the Karama Agricultural Institute. He loved them. He took special care of them. I kneel at their feet. I weep at the feet of the tall trees.

When I think of Antoine, what I feel is not only grief. I feel anger rising up in me. Antoine, the sacrificed. Who sacrificed himself for our sake. He filled the role of the oldest brother, the guardian of the family. Judith had gone away long before. I never saw her at home.

When we were sent to Nyamata, he was alone. André very soon went back to school in Zaza. My father's time was taken up by the refugee camp's day-to-day problems: people came to him for help negotiating with the authorities or settling conflicts, so he couldn't always be there for the family. There was no one but Antoine to help out my mother day to day. I was only four years old, and Julienne just a few months. My mother was pregnant with Jeanne.

In Gitwe, he was the one who cleared the brush so my mother could farm. As I've said, he was the one who went to fetch water, so rare in Bugesera, and he was the one who carried us on his back to the infirmary when we were sick. Did he ever once think of himself? Did he ever think of living his own life, just a little? My mother had to take it upon herself to find him a wife, Jeanne, in Cyugaro, and he set up house as close by my parents' as he could, so he could watch over us. Every day he stopped by to be sure we were well. Antoine was truly alone. In order to earn some money for us, my father had found work in Ngenda with Rutanga, one of Ruvebana's friends, Ruvebana who ran the infirmary. Ngenda was far away, and my father came home only on Sundays. During the week, then, Antoine was the head of the family.

When my father stopped working outside the house, it was Antoine who took over for him. He was hired as a gardener at the Karama Agricultural Institute. At that point, André and Alexia were in secondary school. He earned most of the money that went to our tuition.

My mother was completely dependent on Antoine. He had to do everything. He had a gift for all things manual. He'd taught himself carpentry and furniture-making; people ordered beds from him, he assembled posts and beams for houses. But my mother was proud of Antoine's family above all: nine children, six of them boys. She who had given birth to five girls and only two boys, she believed that thanks to Antoine the future of the family name was guaranteed. Six boys could never all disappear, it was inconceivable. There would surely be a few of them left.

My mother was wrong. Antoine, his wife Jeanne, his nine children, they were all killed. And nothing is left of them, not so much as a name carved into a cross, on a grave. And I walk alone through the tangled thicket that was once their home. And anger wells up in me. Why should that life have been ruined for us? Why should that life have been sacrificed in vain? Antoine, Jeanne, the nine children, nothing left.

I weep in the shadow of the tall trees.

——— ——— ———

The pickup sets off again, and the thickets go by, a little denser as we drive downhill toward the swamps where the lake used to be. I believe I can see shadows hovering in the bright dry-season haze, and among them I'm afraid I might glimpse the faces my memory is calling up.

The face, for example, of Apollinaire Rukema, the deacon who taught catechism after school. He never went out without his Bible under his arm. He and his wife Consessa asked me to be their daughter Jacqueline's godmother. That was in 1973. The ceremony was planned for July. I don't know who took my place.

Across from him lived his brother Haguma, universally respected since he cooked for a white man in Karama. When he married Dafroza, my sister Alexia's godmother, I joined in the evening parties young women traditionally throw for the bride-to-be. Those parties are forbidden to boys, naturally, but also to little girls. I was only nine, but my cousin Mukantwari managed to sneak me in. The parties were held at the girl's parents' house. As soon as they've put away the last cookpot, the young women hurry to the fiancée's. The parents aren't allowed to stay, but they've taken care to set out a few jugs of beer, to keep the party lively. The young women have a wonderful time – they sing, they dance, they tell stories – but the bride has to keep to her bed, weeping and wailing. As the party goes on, her sobs and moans become more and more mournful, until finally the father appears and, brandishing a big stick, pretends to drive out the crowd of young women, who run away, laughing.

This comedy will go on for two weeks, and each evening everyone plays their roles with perfect conviction.

There was also Gakwaya. His wife was named Skolastika, like me. He'd been a chief in Ruhengeri. He thought it beneath his dignity to farm, and he nobly endured hunger in the impeccable drapery of his white *pagne*. We could hear him coming from far away thanks to his creaking old shoes; their badly worn soles gave him a limp. But he refused to wear the sandals all the other refugees made for themselves from old tires. His shoes' shredded leather was all he had left of his former splendor.

Kabugu, too, was of very high birth – he was an Umuhindiro, from the inner circle of kings – but he'd fared better. He'd married one of his daughters to a white man, and from that marriage he'd got a fine house, and better yet a bicycle, which seemed tiny when the very tall Kabugu straddled it.

Then came Bernard, who worked as a cook in Karama, like Haguma. He'd adopted his employers' habits: to the amazement of all, he drank tea every morning, which earned him a place among the great men of Gitagata in spite of his small stature. He'd suffered a terrible loss. His three oldest daughters had died in the same year of a mysterious illness. For a long time, his wife Joséphine bore no other children. Nobody wanted to spend too much time with them. Later, she gave birth to many more children. Relieved, everyone observed that they were in good health. People took to visiting Joséphine again.

Somewhere around here, too, must be the house of Berkimasse, the only tailor in Gitwe and Gitagata. Everyone admired him. We little girls used to hang around his sewing machine. Sometimes, but not often, he would give us a few scraps of fabric to dress our corn- or banana-leaf dolls. Ordering clothes from him was an almost unthinkable luxury, because he refused to accept beans or bananas as payment. He only wanted money. It should be said, all the same, that he was generous with credit, especially for school uniforms: a blue dress for the girls, a khaki shirt and shorts for the boys.

The tailor's sister-in-law Sisiliya had something all the children coveted in her yard. She'd planted two sugar canes. That was a rarity at the time. We all dreamed of chewing the sweet stalks. We were prepared to do her any favor she asked if it would earn us a little piece of cane. Sometimes, on the way to school, we stood for many minutes gazing on the sugar canes, like little Europeans before a candy shop. Sisiliya lived alone with her three children. Her husband had gone to Burundi.

Then there was Patrice. His daughter Patricia sold tomatoes and palm oil at the market. She kept some of the money to buy second-hand clothes. All the girls were jealous of her.

And here, I believe, lived Diyonisi. His wife Raheri's breasts came down almost to her thighs; we called them *imivungavunga*, from the name of a long spongy pod, the fruit of a tree whose name I don't know. His daughter Jacqueline was a classmate of mine, a real friend. The poor thing struggled hard to learn her lessons, but she didn't pass the national exam. She stayed in the village. She's one of the few survivors from Gitagata.

And then Nastasiya, Gakwaya, and Suzanne. Her daughter Colomba talked as loudly as a man. But of course, after her father left for Burundi, she had to become the head of her family . . .

And I must also speak of Sematama, the shame of the village. A high-born Tutsi, he'd abandoned his first wife, the beautiful Stéphanie, and lived with a Hutu woman, Kankera, who'd given him many sons. Those boys were little hoodlums. They didn't go to school, and everyone was shocked by their crude language. And then there was the affair of the stolen cows. Sematama teamed up with some Batwa to steal his neighbor Kabugu's cows! They spent a whole night tramping through the bush in search of a hiding place for the purloined cows. At dawn, early risers found Sematama and his gang of Batwa driving Kabugu's cows along before them. Sematama was pitifully dragging himself along; his legs were badly swollen. They went to tell Kabugu, who, with the whole village helping, captured Sematama and one of his accomplices. They tied the thieves to a tree in Kabugu's yard. It was a beautiful sight, something no one wanted to miss: the noble Sematama tied up with the Batwa! The children danced around the tree, and the whole village walked by, spitting on the culprits' feet. Then the punishment was decided on. To make amends, Sematama offered to invite all of Gitagata to come and drink beer at his house, as much beer as at a wedding. Everyone agreed to share the beer of reconciliation, and Sematama regained at least a little of his respectability.

And who will remember Joséphine Kabanene, the most elegant girl in the village, but also the proudest? When she agreed to dance at a wedding, people came running from far away to watch her shake her beautiful undulating hair. They applauded when she lifted her pretty arms to evoke an inyambo cow's perfect horns. Joséphine did her best to barricade herself in against the young men of the Parmehutu, but more than anything I believe her mother, who sold Primus, bought her daughter's safety with a few bottles of beer. In Bugesera, beer was rarer than pretty girls. The beautiful Kabanene, for her part, refused every marriage proposal, believing that no dowry could be worthy of her beauty. Nonetheless, she ended up marrying a rich shopkeeper from Kigali, who offered the right price.

But I wouldn't want to forget Rutetereza, an albino, more or less thought of as the village idiot. He lived alone with his bedridden grandparents. He was the nicest, most helpful boy I ever knew. Not only did he look after his grandmother, but he was always ready to help out all the old ladies of Gitagata. He fetched their water and wood. He never rested, never complained. He always wore a big smile. My mother was very fond of Rutetereza, she thought of herself as something like his godmother . . .

———— ———— ————

The truck has stopped. To the left of the road, still the same tangle of bushes, of thickets. "Look," Emmanuel says to me, "don't you recognize it? That's Cosma's place, and Stefania's, that's where you lived!" I look at the tangled mass of brush, I have a hard time convincing myself: this is where I lived! "Look," Emmanuel goes on, "there are the sisal plants at the entrance!" Yes, at the edge of the road, there are indeed a few browned leaves, with black spines, slightly withered by the dry weather. Emmanuel points to a tree smothered by brambles and vines: "There's Jeanne's avocado tree!" This is my home, I tell myself over and over, and I realize that, to protect myself, despite everything my brother had told me, everything I knew, I'd clung to the illusion, like a deep secret hope, that the ruination of Gitagata had spared something in the place where I once lived, that some sign was awaiting me from beyond death's realm. But of course there was no one and nothing. And suddenly I began to violently hate the untamed vegetation that had so efficiently finished the murderers' "work," that had turned my home into this inhospitable patch of brush. I don't want to listen to Emmanuel's explanations. I don't want to answer my son's questions. I don't want to know where the old house was, or the new one. I am alone in a foreign land, where no one is waiting for me.

I close my eyes, and on memory's stage, all the vanished things reappear and take their place. Here are the big coffee plants, covered with red berries, greeting me at the entrance again. I love walking barefoot on the carpet of dried-grass mulch all around them. The path is lined with yellow flowers, lovingly tended by Jeanne. Just by the house, the banana trees grow strong on the beans' cooking liquid: they bear the most succulent varieties – the *kamaramasenge*, the *ikingurube*. My mother has saved up the nicest bunches, waiting for vacation to come, when we'll be home again. A tall cassava tree serves as an awning before the front door. My mother is waiting for me on the threshold. She's tied on her finest *pagne*, the one she wears for Mass. We give each other a long embrace, as custom dictates, as if to fill each other with the warmth of our bodies. She leads me inside, and I hear the familiar bubbling of the sorghum beer fermenting in the big jugs. We walk into the dark room. My mother hands me a straw. I thrust it into the sparkling liquid. I'm home.

It's not easy, but I find a way through the *ibihehaheha*, those bushes whose hollow stems we use as straws. They've taken everything over. Then the thicket turns less dense, I cross a patch of bare land: this is our old field. Its edge is still marked by an *umucyuro*, whose leaves are good for skin diseases. We always took great care to spare them when we were clearing brush. I realize that I'm following a very visible path, evidently still used. I even come across a field of sweet potatoes and papaya plants. And suddenly I find myself at the entry of an enclosure hidden up to now by a hollow in the terrain: the main house, rectangular, made of pounded earth, and then a few smaller huts, cruder, perhaps stables or children's shacks, the yard carefully swept. A friendly-looking woman comes toward my husband, who's walking ahead, but when she catches sight of me behind him she lets out a cry and runs off. I can still hear her in the banana grove, on the slope of the Gikombe valley, wailing again and again: "*Yebabawe! Yebabawe! Karabaye!* – It had to happen! It had to happen!"

I see a little girl crouching in the narrow band of shadow at the foot of the big hut's wall. I ask her: "Who is that woman? Why did she run away?" She doesn't know her, she's a neighbor who'd come calling. And then, without my having asked her anything, she goes on: "You know, I'm twelve years old, I was too little during the war, I didn't see anything." She breaks off there. A man has appeared in the doorway, and now he's coming toward us. I recognize him at once: yes, that's him, the neighbor my mother invited to "my party" in 1986. I ask him who used to live next door. No one, he first insists: "On the other side of the road, yes, there were people there, that was Munyaneza's house, but no one ever lived next door to me." What about Cosma? He's never heard of Cosma. Then he corrects himself: oh yes, of course, Cosma, but when that happened he wasn't there, he was in the Congo.

"Listen," Emmanuel says to him, "this is Cosma's daughter in front of you, do you have anything to say to her?"

A long silence. He hesitates.

"Yes, that's Cosma's daughter, now that I see her, I can certainly ask for her forgiveness . . . "

I stand glued to the spot, half-paralyzed, stunned by these words. Another long silence, and then I search in vain for some way of encouraging him to go on, to tell me what I've so long wanted to know . . . But it's already too late, he's gone back to his denials, I'll get nothing more out of him.

"Listen, I never killed anyone, they went up there to Rebero, I didn't kill anyone. It was around four in the afternoon when they left, I remember. I didn't kill anyone. Have you ever heard anyone say I did? The family died on Rebero. They were old. No one died here. I never met his children, except for that day he married off his last daughter . . . "

I'm no longer listening. Was it him who murdered my parents, who'd at least played a part? Was it someone else? I'll never know.

But I don't give up. I don't want to leave without some sort of sign. I feel like I have to show I'm still here, still alive. Have I carried out the mission my parents entrusted me with thirty years before? To live, in the name of all the others. I who had no choice but to be a good Catholic schoolgirl, I begin to hope that the spirit of the dead –

the *umuzimu* – will appear in the brush, in what's left of the banana grove, and give me an answer.

Here in the midst of the thicket, I believe I can make out the spot where we gathered in the evening, the hearth with its three stones set in the wide, flat clay dish – the *urubumbiro* – shaped by my mother. My father is there reading his Bible by the light of the hurricane lantern. Near the hearth, the three of us, Jeanne, Julienne, and I, are pressed in around Mama, listening to her stories. And indeed, under the intertwining branches, I find a little pile of gravel and stones. As if driven by an unknown force, I sweep away a few pebbles. A black snake slithers out from the stones, then disappears into the tall grass. And I who am terrified of snakes, I find myself not crying out, not fleeing as fast as my legs will carry me. Fascinated, my eyes are glued to the serpent's coils as it makes its silent way among the dried branches.

I walk to the pickup, my thoughts endlessly going back to the snake. Strangely, the sight of it seems almost to have comforted me and brought me a feeling of peace. This isn't the deadly snake coiled in the banana grove. It isn't the snake whose name the Hutus spat at us as an insult. Nor is it the serpent in my father's Bible, the one they showed us in church, wrapped around the branch of the tree in paradise. This is the snake my mother knew all about, she who knew so many things that the missionaries' oppressive teachings forbade her to pass on, but that sometimes, poking out through a sentence or a gesture – often addressed to me – revealed a whole world hidden beneath the lessons of the catechism: "Before," she would say, "before the white people came, every enclosure had its own familiar snake, and it was respected because it alone knew the way to the land of the spirits of the dead, and when we saw it we thought it was a sign of their good wishes."

I would so like to think that this snake was a sign sent by all those who perished, that they were telling me I hadn't betrayed my family, that I'd had to follow the long detour of exile for their sake, that I'd come back to answer their call and shoulder the memory of their sufferings and their deaths. Yes, I am indeed the one they called by her Rwandan name, the one given me by my father, Mukasonga, but now, deep inside, like the most precious part of me, I hold what's left of the lives and the names of all those in Gitwe and Gitagata and Cyohoha who will never be properly buried. The murderers tried to erase everything they were, even any memory of their existence, but, in the schoolchild's notebook that I am now never without, I write down their names. I have nothing left of my family and all the others who died in Nyamata but that paper grave.

archipelago books

is a not-for-profit literary press devoted to
promoting cross-cultural exchange through innovative
classic and contemporary international literature
www.archipelagobooks.org